Dr. David Yonggi CHO

MW01067687

Dr. David Yonggi CHO

Ministering Hope for 50 Years

BRIDGE LOGOS FOUNDATION

Alachua, Florida 32615

Bridge-Logos
Alachua, FL 32615 USA

Dr. David Yonggi Cho, Ministering Hope for 50 Years
by Dr. David Yonggi Cho
Institute for Church Growth, Seoul, South Korea

Copyright ©2008 by Bridge-Logos

This book or parts thereof may not be reproduced in any form, stored in a retrieval system or transmitted in any form by any means—electronic, mechanical, photocopy, recording or otherwise—without prior written permission of the publisher, except as provided by United States of America copyright law.

Printed in the United States of America.

Library of Congress Catalog Card Number: 2008924069
International Standard Book Number 978-0-88270-480-7

Scripture quotations marked KJV are taken from the *King James Version* of the Bible.

Scripture quotations marked NIV are taken from the *Holy Bible: New International Version*. Copyright © 1973, 1978, 1984 by International Bible Society. Used by permission of Zondervan Publishing House. All rights reserved.

Scripture quotations marked NKJV are taken from the *New King James Version*. Copyright © 1982 by Thomas Nelson, Inc. Used by permission. All rights reserved.

G410.317.B.m804.35220

Contents

Part 1 — Page 1

A Sickly Teenage Boy Meets Jesus

Part 2 — Page 17

Growth of the Tent Church

Part 3 — Page 65

Ministry in Seodaemun Church and the Encounter with the Holy Spirit

Part 4 — Page 105

The World's Largest Church

Part 5 — Page 129

A Ministry That Extends Out to the World

Dr. Cho's family when Dr. Cho was four years old.

Part 1

A Sickly Teenage Boy Meets Jesus

The Death Sentence Announcement

In 1950, there was a war in our country between North Korea and South Korea that lasted approximately two years. It was called the Korean War. Bombs from that war destroyed buildings, homes, and schools in every mountain, plain, and city in our country, and many people were killed or injured throughout Korea. There were also many heartbreaking family separations that took place. People led difficult lives of poverty and hunger even after the war ended.

My story starts here. My hometown is Kyungsangnam-do Uljugun Seonammyun Kyodongni. I was a mischievous, energetic, young boy with many dreams, and I was on my elementary school's baseball team. When I was at Dongnae Middle School in Busan, I was a brightly smiling adolescent who knew how to appreciate the melody of the birds that seemed to sing about dreams and the refreshing wind. When I entered high school, even though we were in hard times, I would visit the nearby United States Army Base and learn English from the soldiers. I worked various odd jobs after school to earn my tuition, and I was always happy as I worked, because I had many dreams of a bright future in my mind.

While walking to school one morning, I saw two men, one of whom I often worked for, and I said, "Hello Sir! I think I will be able to help you after school today."

"Sure," he said, then he turned to the other man with him and said, "What an energetic and honest lad!"

"He sure is!" the other man replied.

I worked hard every day and heard compliments that I was diligent and smart due to the English that I learned from the U.S. soldiers. Then one day something unexpected happened to me. I was in my second year of high school (eleventh grade), and I was working as a private tutor to a young student. Suddenly, blood started pouring out of my nose and mouth, and I eventually passed out because the blood continued without stopping. I was seventeen at the time.

To save me, my shocked parents hurriedly took me to the largest and most well-known hospital in the area. At the hospital they took X-rays and drew blood samples from my arm. I had many tests, and finally after several days, the doctor told us, "The results of the tests are back, and unfortunately, it is tuberculosis."

The moment we heard this, everything turned dark for my parents and me; it was as if we had been hit hard over the head with something. "I have tuberculosis?" I said. "The disease that kills everyone that contracts it?" I could not believe it. These days tuberculosis is curable through treatment; but during that time it was a scary, incurable disease. "Is there really no treatment?" I asked. "I just have to wait as I get sicker and sicker and die? Doctor, please save me. I don't want to die like that. Isn't there anything you can do to save me?"

Dr. Cho's family when Dr. Cho was in elementary school.

Turning slightly away from me, the doctor said, "As of right now, Yonggi, there is no treatment. There is nothing I can do. You have maybe three months, four at the most, to live. It is unfortunate, but the best thing for you to do is go home, eat everything you desire, do whatever you want to do, and say your farewells to your friends and family."

After hearing this, I began to cry, "I still have so much I want to do, and they're telling me I am going to die! I still have dreams. Why do I have to die? This isn't true! I still have my studies left, and I need to work and make money." I was very sad about my helpless situation.

After returning to my parent's home, I marked an "X" on the calendar with every passing day. "Another day has passed!" I said to myself, "There's only two months and twenty-nine days left for me to see the warm sun and bright moon." I marked an "X"

3

Dr. Cho was on the baseball team when he was in elementary school.

on the calendar the next day, and the day after that, and as the "Xs" increased, my desire to live also increased. Then I thought, "Maybe if I go to a Buddhist temple and pray, I will be cured!" With that thought in mind, I went and prayed to Buddha. But my disease continued to worsen rather than improve, and I even threw up blood as I coughed from the pain in my chest.

Then I thought of something else, maybe I should ask the God that my friends believe in to save me? As a last resort, I decided to look to the God I did not know. I cried out, "God, I want to live! I want to live! Please help me!" My weak voice grew louder as my emotions overcame me. At the time, I really didn't think the words that I spoke in desperation would become a life-changing moment. Also, I didn't think that God was with me while I was praying, but when I think about it now, I believe that God was with me in my small, dark room and listening to my prayer.

The Girl Who Walked Through the Twig Gates
Soon after that, an unexpected guest came to my home. "Is anyone home?" I heard a voice say, and then the gate opened and a girl in a high school uniform came in.

"Who is it?" I asked in a weak voice. To anyone who saw me it was obvious that I was very sick.

"Hi," she said. "You're a student also. You look sick. Do you want me to help you?" She walked up to me and introduced herself as a high school student like me, and told me that she would like to tell me about the most important person in the world. And then she started to talk about God, the same God that I had prayed to a few days before. She said, "I'm going to tell you about God and His Son, Jesus. Because God loved us so much, He sent His Son, Jesus, to us to save us from our sins. Jesus came down to this world and healed many sick people and sinners. Then He was crucified and died on the Cross with our sins, curses, and diseases on His shoulders, and after three days in death, He rose from the dead. If you will believe in Jesus, He will save you for certain. So, please! Believe in Jesus."

The pretty girl that suddenly appeared before me started telling me about the gospel in a calm and sure manner; however, to me, who was hearing the gospel for the first time, it all seemed like a wild lie. So I told the girl in an irritated voice, "That's a lie! Don't lie to me. I'm not in the mood to listen to your lies, and I don't even have the strength to talk. Leave! The things you said about God's Son don't even make any sense, and I've never seen a person as weird as you are! So leave! And don't go around saying things like that anymore."

The next day, the girl returned. She carefully opened the gate, and just like yesterday, she was in her school uniform as if she had come straight from school. "Why are you here again?" I asked sternly.

"Hello! How are you today?" she replied. "When I went home yesterday, I prayed to God for you, and while I was praying for you, I really felt God's love for you, and I started crying for you even though I don't know you very well. God is a loving God, and it seems to me that He has a special love for you. God wants to save you, but you can only be saved if you believe in His Son, Jesus. I know this, because why else would I have prayed for you and even started crying? I know it's because God loves you very much." After telling me this, she started to share the gospel with me just as she had the day before. She did the same the next day, and the day after that. She came to me every day—that was very strange.

While I was telling myself not to believe the girl's stories, I found I still wanted to hear more of what she had to say, and I couldn't rid my mind of the stories that she had told me. I kept thinking, "What's wrong with me? Why do I keep on thinking about this Jesus person? No!" I yelled at myself, "stop it mind—I don't want to think of Him." During such times I would shake my head and try to get God out of my mind.

A week passed, and every day that week the girl came at the same time to talk to me about the gospel. I was very irritable and in a weak physical state, however, and I spoke to the girl in anger, "Hey! I don't want to listen to what you're saying! I don't believe in Jesus! I don't need Jesus, and I don't need you telling me what to believe, so stop coming! Don't you dare come back here again!"

But to my surprise, the girl was not ashamed or humiliated at my anger as I expected her to be, she just knelt down without saying anything and brought her hands together and started to pray sincerely to her God. "Lord! Please save my friend. Please cure him from the disease that is ailing him, and please have mercy on him. Let him know Jesus. Oh, Jesus ..." The girl who had suddenly started praying had tears coming down her pale cheeks. I could not help being surprised, for no one had sympathized with my pain before, yet here was this girl, who I had just yelled at in anger, praying for me. I was in awe and grateful to her. Then everything in my mind became very complicated and I thought "What is wrong with this girl? Why is she crying for me? Who am I that she is crying and praying for me? And what is this heavy feeling in my heart?" I believe that it was at this time that my frozen heart began to thaw with the love of Jesus, and I didn't know how I was supposed to respond.

I had a strange feeling of someone knocking at my heart's door as the girl was praying for me, and this feeling had me transfixed for a long time. Then I slowly opened my mouth after a long silence and said, "Please, don't cry. I'm sorry. I will believe! I will at least try. You made me want to get to know this Jesus. Really. So please stop crying."

When she heard me speak, she wiped away her tears and a bright smile appeared on her face as if she had never been crying, and she said, "Really? You're really going to believe in Jesus?" She started jumping in joy, and she shouted toward heaven, "Thank you, God! Thank you so much. Thank you for taking him in as your child." She took my bony hands, and placed the Bible that she carried in them, and happily said to me, "Read this Bible from now on, because you will be able to meet God when you read it, and you will also be cured of your disease for certain!"

The book that the young girl placed in my hand was the first Bible that I had ever touched. My heart started racing when I laid eyes on it. Whew! I let out my breath, and carefully opened the first page of the Bible expecting great things; however, the Bible was not fun to read. It was full of names about who begot who, it was like hearing my family, especially the women, talk about so and so, who begot so and so, and who begot who. I was really disappointed and said to the girl, "Why is this like this! You told me I could meet God if I read this. This book is all about people's genealogies. I'd rather read the phone directory. I don't want to read the Bible!"

She calmly replied, "I know it doesn't seem to be as interesting as I told you it would be right now, but as you keep reading it you will begin to understand about the people with those names, what they did and what happened to them. Then you will find that the Bible is so interesting and even fun to read, that you won't want to put it down. So don't give up. Okay?" she said, smiling encouragingly. I received courage from her words and picked up the book and opened it as if nothing happened.

Meeting the Bible

The Bible, which I held in my hands for the first time, seemed to be talking to me, "Please, open me. Please read me." I began to wonder about the contents of this book. "What is it trying to say to me?" I thought. My curiosity and expectations led me to read the first page. Inside the Bible, I read many touching stories, and there were eye-opening and breathtakingly shocking truths waiting to be found in this book. The main character of this book was Jesus, the Son of God. With Jesus as the focus of this book, I realized that God was writing a love letter to the world. The contents of this love letter were letting us know that by believing in Jesus we can have salvation and become a new person as a child of God.

As I was reading the Bible, my head started to fill with thoughts about Jesus. "Jesus, who is free of sin, is the Son of God! Jesus died on the Cross to save people from their sins. We can receive salvation by just believing in Jesus, and we can overcome poverty and illness, which is impossible with just human will. Wow! This is so wonderful!"

I read about how Jesus took pity on sick people and cured them. Then I thought "In the Bible, there is no disease that Jesus can't cure! If this is true, does that mean that Jesus will cure me for certain? Then I will live and be healthy again!" Before reading the Bible, I lived my life in fear of death and despair, but the words of the Bible gave me a light of hope. I was able to have expectations of living again, all because of what I read in the Bible.

I could also feel God's love for me as I read the stories in the Bible, and then suddenly, I was on my knees praying to God, and there were hot tears falling from my eyes as I cried out, "Lord! Thank you for loving a sinner like me. Thank you for loving a diseased person like me. I've sinned all this time because I did not know of your love and Jesus' salvation. Please forgive me. Please forgive me." While I was praying and crying out to God in tears, my life of sin crossed before my eyes like a movie. I could not stop the tears, and the more I cried, the more I could feel God's warmth surrounding my heart.

Meeting Jesus

I met Jesus as I read the Bible, and then miraculous things started happening in my life. Even though I was sick, I read the Bible every day. The Words of the Bible were refreshing like ice cream and deliciously sweet like chocolate, and the more I read, the more I wanted to read and learn and understand. And yes, just as the girl had said, I wanted to read it more and more and I found it was even fun to read.

When I read how Jesus opened the eyes of Bartimaeus, a blind man, and cured a person who suffered from paralysis for thirty-eight years, a lump started in my throat and I felt the stories were true. When I read about how Jesus raised Lazarus from the dead, I felt that I, too, could live, if Jesus cured me from tuberculosis.

The thought of dying melted in my head like snow and was replaced with, "I will be able to live, if Jesus cures me! In fact, I do believe Jesus will be able to heal me." Jesus had filled my heart with this belief and I began to grow in happiness day by day. This all happened because of the girl who came through the gate and introduced me to Jesus just a few days before. When I think about it now, I know Jesus himself visited me through the girl.

Six months after that incident, God presented me with a very big miracle. The doctors had told me that I only had three more months to live but I was still alive six months later, and feeling lighter and definitely healthier. The tuberculosis that had been weighing me down gradually disappeared from my body after I started believing that Jesus would cure me. I knelt on my knees and prayed as I thought about the changes in me and in my body, all because of the positive thoughts that God put inside my head. "Thank you God. I praise the Lord. I thank you for forgiving me of my sins and curing me from my disease."

Even my severe cough disappeared. As I recovered my healthy state, and read and reread the Bible I began to think, *What can I do for Jesus, who saved me and cured me?* In the Bible I read that everyone that meets Jesus ends up becoming a disciple and starts introducing the people around them to Jesus. I know what I can do—like the disciples I, too, will become a person who lets the world know about Jesus. I'll share this touching experience I've had with the world and let them know about Jesus who saved me."

My parents were the first ones I introduced to God. I told them every single detail about what happened to me and why I was able to live. I also told them I was resolved to work as a disciple of Jesus from then on. At the time I was still a high school student, so my parents and the rest of the family did not fully agree with my decision, but in 1956 I left my hometown for Seoul. I felt like Abraham, who left his hometown of Ur of the Chaldees under the guidance of God. Then I enrolled in the Full Gospel Seminary.

Doing My Best in Seminary

After enrolling in seminary, I prayed and studied a lot harder. As I thought about it, I said to myself, *Learning about God really makes me happy! I will ask the Reverend Johnston, my teacher, to tell me some more Bible stories tomorrow, and I must also teach him how to speak Korean.* I was very busy, and I was very happy! I had learned English from the U.S soldiers, so I was able to translate the Reverend Johnston's English into Korean for the students. I was the student body president, and in that position it was my responsibility to lead the students.

One day I heard someone shout to me, "Student body President Cho! What are we going to do today?" It was Jasil Choi, who had become a student during her forties and was in charge of evangelism in the seminary. As a middle-aged lady, Jasil Choi was the oldest student in the seminary. She was more like a warm mother to all the students, and a mother figure to me also.

"We're going to go witnessing today," I replied. "We are going out to the streets to tell the people of the gospel. I know it's going to be a bit embarrassing, but I also know the Holy

Dr. Cho with his youths standing in line for lunch during a revival meeting.

11

Spirit will help us, so let's go Sister Choi!" Even though I was enthusiastic I got butterflies in my stomach every time we went out on the streets carrying our drums, beating them with our hands and witnessing.

We had boarded the bus to go to the streets, when the bus driver turned and yelled at us, "Hey! You're going to have to get off. You can't beat those drums like that inside the bus. Hurry up and get off! Right now!" Sometimes we couldn't even get on the bus with our big drums because the bus drivers were bad tempered.

As we got off the bus I said to the students, "Let's walk to Pagoda Park. God has given us strong legs, it will be easy for us!"

"That's right!" Sister Choi and the rest of the students agreed. I smiled and said, "Yes, it will be fun too, so start beating your drums! Let the people know that the Army of Heaven is here with good news!" The conversation between the students and the student body president was filled with happiness.

The sound of the drums attracted the children of the town first, then the people gathered to listen to the gospel. They were very poor and sad, but I saw them as beautiful people of God as I exclaimed joyfully to them, "We are here with good news, and we are here to bring you hope! Hear our good news, believe in Jesus and be blessed. Doctors told me that I would die of tuberculosis, but look at me standing here before you, healthy, fit and totally cured of tuberculosis, because I believed in Jesus and He healed me. You too will be blessed if you believe in Jesus. So listen to our good news, it will fill you with hope and help you believe in Jesus!"

We passed on hope to the people. That was the first step in my path toward God's calling, and even though it was hard work, I still feel energized and smile when I think about those happy times. After that, wherever I went, I told people of my touching first meeting with Jesus. My one wish then, and now, is for everyone to receive the gift of God's salvation.

Answering the Call to Ministry

During my years in the seminary, I dreamed of becoming a theologian. I wanted to become a professor who trained and cultivated well-equipped pastors, and set up a college and graduate school to train the next generation. So my priority in those days was teaching Korean to the Reverend Johnston and continuing my preparation to go to America. My plan was to leave soon after I graduated.

One Wednesday, after the first snowfall of the year, it was unusually cold as the temperature had dropped below freezing. That kind of weather was unbearable for someone like me; because of once having tuberculosis I was still physically weak. Then I became extremely ill and was diagnosed with acute pneumonia. I developed a high fever over 40° Celsius (104° Fahrenheit), and the doctor warned me that my life might be in danger.

The dorm rooms had plywood partitions and straw mats on the floor, and the cold lingered in my straw mat covered only with an old blanket. I had only a thin blanket to wrap around myself, so it was almost unbearably cold. I had been fighting this lingering illness without food for four days, and now, groaning and moaning, I felt like I had no strength to live. Then someone paid me a visit. Under the dim lights I couldn't make out who it was at first, then I saw that it was Jasil Choi (Lay Minister Choi), the leader of a witnessing team from church. Laying her hands on me, she said, "How are you doing? Have you had anything to eat yet?"

I had no energy to speak, as I stared at her with my bloodshot eyes and unwillingly closed them. Jasil Choi was a retired nurse, so she gave me a shot of fever reducer, and fed me some heat-steamed dumplings and soup. I drank the soup to the very last drop and immediately vomited everything I had eaten, and collapsed. I guess my stomach, which had been inactive for four days, went into a bit of a shock. Then, I lost consciousness.

I realized years later, that had it not been for Lay Minister Choi, who is like a mother to me, and her care, nursing and prayers, along with those of other men and women of prayer, I would have never recuperated from that condition. I was back on my feet again with improved health, and I was so grateful to her and her fellow prayer warriors, that one day I went and asked her to become my spiritual mentor as well as a mother figure to me.

This experience led me to do some very deep and extensive soul-searching. I discovered that my desires of becoming a pastor and minister to those who were poverty-stricken and desperately in need had withered away. I saw myself as now being an ambitious person chasing after a dream to gain an honorable status as a professor, rather than leading the hard and tough life of a pastor. My mind was preoccupied with going to America to achieve that dream so that I could bring glory to myself, and I knew that such thoughts were irreconcilable before God, so right then I confessed to God all of my deep dark secrets and doings. After that wake-up call, I stopped thinking about studying in America and poured my time and energy into reading the Bible and theology books to discover God's plan for my life. I devoted much passion toward prayers as well. Quite frequently, I climbed up Samkak Mountain with my classmates from the seminary to receive the anointing of the Holy Spirit.

In October 1957, a world-renowned American evangelist and pastor, H. Herman, held twenty-four days of revival meetings on the Capitol Plaza. I was asked to be the interpreter. The time was ripe for people to hear messages of hope and blessing to comfort their pains and bitterness from the war, so swarms of people flocked to the place, and the Holy Spirit moved powerfully. While I was interpreting I didn't feel like myself, I felt as if I was possessed by something—it certainly wasn't the real me. I even spoke louder than the evangelist, and then found out some time later that many people who attended the revival were a bit stunned because they couldn't tell who the real preacher was. That's how passionate I was.

Every night of the revival, many of the seminary students flocked to the plaza for all-night prayers to prepare their hearts to receive more blessings. When the temperature dipped late in the night, the students gathered straw bags and threw them over their bodies to stay warm while praying. I joined my fellow seminarians, in spite of my tiredness and physical condition. They pleaded with me to rest since I had to serve as the interpreter, but I didn't listen as I delved even deeper into prayer. Through these experiences, I began realizing that my calling had been to become a pastor, rather than a scholar all along, and without a doubt these hardships fortified my physical body.

This abandoned U.S. military tent on the hilltops of Daejo-dong was where the most amazing story of church growth began.

Part 2

The Growth of the Tent Church

The Apple Box Pulpit

On Wednesday, May 18, 1958, we held our church's inauguration service, our first group meeting. One morning just prior to the meeting, I saw Lay Minister Choi working very diligently on something. I said, "Mother, what are you doing this early in the morning?" I called Lay Minister Choi *mother* when we first started the church. That is because she was about the same age as my mother who was back home, and she always prayed for me like a mother. "What are you doing with the apple crates?" I asked.

"Lay Minister Cho," she replied. "I'm sure these apple crates will come to good use today. You'll see." Lay Minister Mother connected the apple crates into one long block, turned them on end, and draped a cloth over the crates. "See! We just made a pulpit. Pretty nice isn't it?" she said, laughing.

"Mother!" I said, "that is really nice, and since you made it, it's the one and only Mother-brand pulpit," We laughed together about it then and many times after through our years together. We were so happy as we prepared for our first service since officially starting the church.

A few weeks before our inauguration service, Sister Choi went out in the neighborhood to witness. She reached out to people any way she could; she would go out into the fields to help people pick peppers or green onions and even to pull out weeds. If lending a hand on the fields seemed unnecessary, she would baby sit with their children, or sing hymns to the people. Gradually their hearts began to soften, proving the effectiveness of her deeds and resulting in five confirmations from people that they would attend the service. One day when she went out, five people promised to attend our first official service—we also hoped others would come, since we had told many about our new church.

I had prepared a message, and I didn't have to be at the tent until seven, but I got there an hour early and ran up the hill gasping and panting. I was greeted by a feast that Mother Choi fixed for me, and after dinner I began preparing for the service. No one showed up, not even the ones who had promised to come. At eight o'clock, rain started pouring down and there was still no sign of any people. Sister Choi said in an apologetic and disappointed voice, "I'm sorry, Lay Minister Cho. I guess the five aren't going to show up."

"That's all right," I said. "Let's just trust in God."

The total number of people who attended the service that evening was, Lay Minister Choi, her three children, and me. Instead of the five who had promised to show up, there were the five of us. So I guess numerically speaking five people did attend our inauguration service that night. We sang hymns together, and even though the number was small, I had faith in our Lord's promise that where two or more are gathered together, He will be there as well. I envisioned a day when this church would be filled with hundreds of church members.

After the hymns, I read from God's Word, "And these signs shall follow them that believe; in my name shall they cast out devils; they shall speak with new tongues; They shall take up serpents; and if they drink any deadly thing, it shall not hurt them; they shall lay hands on the sick, and they shall recover" (Mark 16:17-18, KJV) "Do you believe in these words?" I asked. "If you do, say 'Amen.'"

"Amen," they responded. But their *Amen* had no enthusiasm or vigor.

Then I said, "Let's pray together: Lord, there are many who live in this neighborhood but not one showed up this evening. But I envision thirty, sixty, and one hundred. The Word of the Lord says, 'As you believe, it shall come to pass ... Open your mouth wide, I shall fill it ... Those who don't dream shall perish.' Therefore, we believe this hour that everyone residing in Daejo-dong will come to believe in the Lord. We pray this in the name of Jesus. Amen."

I was so overwhelmed with His power and anointing that the room with so few people did not even enter my sight. My heart was filled with the living Jesus Christ working among us, and in a strong voice I began proclaiming the Word of God in a message titled Signs that Accompany Believers: "Our Lord came to earth to destroy the devil's work. He healed the woman who had the issue of blood for twelve years; raised Lazarus from death, exorcised evil spirits, helped those in need, and performed healings wherever He went. That same Jesus who is alive today and works among us is the same yesterday, today and forever. Believe in Jesus Christ. Accept Him into your life. Those who believe shall be accompanied by signs following them. You will experience a change of heart, illnesses and poverty shall disappear, and evil spirits shall depart." Just as excitement began to build from the powerful sermon, the door opened, and a stooped over old woman came in holding a bamboo basket in her hand. She shouted "Hey, Hallelujah Lady, I'm here. Were you waiting for me?"

Lay Minister Choi, who many of the villagers called "Hallelujah Lady" because she was so enthusiastic about the things of God, forgot that she was in the middle of our service and yelled out exuberantly, "Welcome, grandma! It's so good to see you!"

After sitting the old woman down, I continued my message, and even though I spoke before only an uneducated old lady and a family of four, I was filled with joy and excitement. With just a taste of what ministry was like, my plan to go to America to earn my doctorate degree was dissipating rapidly as I looked toward God's calling to ministry.

Desk and Chair Ordered Through Prayer

I looked around the room I used as my church office, it was such a small room. In this room no one waited for me, nor was there any furniture. It was just an empty space with silence as my only friend. This was during the time after I graduated from seminary and was spreading the gospel with passion. One day someone said to me "Pastor! You must have had a hard day. Where did you go today?"

"Today I went to a village about four kilometers away to witness. Tomorrow I will go out a little farther." I replied.

"You're working very hard," the person said. And I was. During that time, to spread word about Jesus, I would travel many miles until my feet were swollen; however, I was still happy and my heart swelled with joy. One day, the same as any

Dr. Cho with the witch-turned-believer (center) and mother-in-law Choi (right).

other day, I was coming back after spreading the word about Jesus. The sun was hanging over the mountains, and then the clouds suddenly covered it. I thought to myself as I gazed at this magnificent sight, "The sky looks so picturesque in the setting sun. It's so awesome looking. Just look at that colorful sun! It seems like God painted this sunset just to cheer me on. Thank you Lord!"

After I was done witnessing, I arrived home when it was about to get dark. As I changed my clothes, I thought about my day, because in the evening while reading the Bible and talking to the Lord, it was my habit to go over the things that I had done that day. I was reading the New Testament, the part in which Jesus takes His disciples around to spread the gospel to the poor, sick and possessed people. This particular evening, I was reading the Book of John, and there was a verse that really caught my eye. It felt like the size of the text was getting bigger and bigger, and then it seemed like the words were coming to life. It was the first time I had ever experienced such a thing even though I read the Bible often. My heart started pounding, and I heard someone speak to me. "Yet to all who received Him, to those who believed in His name, He gave the right to become children of God." They were the words from John 1:12. Strangely enough, starting from that moment I could not get the thought of "children of God" out of my mind.

"Wow!" I thought, "I am a child of God, God who created the world. I, Yonggi Cho, am a son of God! This is amazing!" As I was meditating on these words, I received confirmation in my heart that I was a child of God. Suddenly, the verse in John 14:14 popped into my head. "You may ask for anything in my name, and I will do it," That means if I ask for anything in the name of God, He will provide it for me. God is my Father, and I am God's son. Meaning, the Father will give His son anything that His son desires. Exactly! At that time I felt like someone gave me an all-access key. My heart was pounding even harder as I knelt in prayer, and discovered God's promises. "God! I believe that the Bible passage I read today was meant for me, your son. Master of the world, you are now my Father. But Lord, I, your son, have nothing right now. Look! I do not even have a desk or chair. I don't have a bike either. I believe that you are the richest in the world. Lord, my Father God, I would like to tell you the things I need. Like you said, 'Ask for anything in my name, and I will do it,' please answer my prayer. Father God! I need a desk to study at. Please give me a desk and chair. I also need a bike for when I witness. Please, also give me a bike. I believe that you, Father God answer your son's needs. I pray in Jesus' name. Amen"

When I finished my prayer, my heart was so full that I felt like I had received a positive answer back from God. Because I truly believed that God would give me the things I needed, I felt like I could see the desk and chair in my room. Just thinking about it made me happy. I could not see those objects with my eyes, but with my heart's eye I believed that the desk and chair were already in my room. I relied on the Word of God every day and waited for the things that I ordered during my prayer. A month and then two months passed, but the items that I ordered in faith did not seem like they would come any time soon. Truthfully, there were seeds of doubt in my mind and I began to question the truth of God's words. But I overcame those doubts and tried very hard to believe that God would give me what I asked for. As faith and doubt played a tug-of-war in my mind, six months passed. Still, my prayer was not answered.

Summer was ending and the fall rain outside was announcing the coming of autumn, and in an instant the doubt in my mind overtook me, and I began to complain, "God! What is this? I asked you many months ago for a desk, chair, and bicycle. Does it make sense that six months have passed and nothing is happening? Lord! You know how difficult it is to witness in this poor village. I have bragged to the village people that my God is a good God who answers our prayers. I am disappointed God." I was so distressed, and in such pain that I did not want to continue God's work. I whined to God just like a kid to his mother. "God! When are you going to fulfill my prayer? I thought you fulfilled all your promises. So why is my prayer from six months ago not being answered. Please hurry!" Hot tears rolled down my face. I prayed and cried for a long time, and then suddenly, I felt God giving me peace. Instantly, the complaints I had toward God vanished.

Then I heard God's voice in a deep corner of my mind, *"Yonggi! I heard your prayer a long time ago."*

"God! Then what happened to my desk, chair, and bicycle?" I asked.

"Yonggi," He replied, *"I would like to answer my children's prayers, quickly, but they do not pray to me in detail and you are the same. There are many types of desks, chairs, and bicycles in the world, and you have never told me clearly and specifically the details of what you need. Tell me what you want and be specific."*

This is what I didn't know! I was shocked. No one had taught me how to pray properly. God then brought to my mind Hebrew 11:1, "Now faith is being sure of what we hope for and certain of what we do not see." I knelt down again and prayed, "God! I am so sorry. I was wrong. I will change the way I pray."

That very day I started to pray in detail, illustrating in my mind what I wanted, and having faith like God told me. "God, I need a desk. I would like it to be of Philippine mahogany, and I would like it to be big enough so that it can fit against the wall with the window. Thank you for giving me a nice desk. I also need a chair, and I would like it to have steel trims, and wheels so I will be able to move freely around my desk. Thank you for giving me a beautiful chair. I need a bicycle. I know there are a lot of types, but I would like an American bike, which is the fastest and strongest. I would also like it to have gears so that I can control the speed. God, thank you for giving me a cool bike." I envisioned everything that I asked for in my prayer in my mind like a picture. I was shaking from joy as I was filled with my dreams after the prayer. That night, I was able to sleep as comfortably as a baby wrapped in its mother's arms.

Just like the last time, a long time passed after I prayed. However, it became a time in which I learned the many ways of God. One must learn how to be patient after praying. Although it could not be seen with my eyes, my faith that God would provide was growing inside me, so I didn't worry. I said to God, "God! The Philippine mahogany desk is really nice. Here is the chair with the wheels next to the desk. I can move around in it easily. God, look at the strong American-made bicycle. It's so sturdy!" Even though there was nothing in my room at the time, I imagined that everything that I had ordered was in my room, and prayed as if they were already there.

I learned more about faith as God trained me during my prayer time, and one day, my prayer was answered. Finally, the items promised by God were delivered to me. A man came to my office door huffing and puffing loudly, and said, "Pastor! Oh, I'm so out of breath from hurrying! I came to tell you that you have a shipment at your home."

"Shipment? I didn't order anything," I said.

"Well I don't know anything about that," he replied, "all I know is there's a shipment, and you should get over there."

When I got to the house and saw the packages I was so surprised that I couldn't close my mouth—the shapes of the things in front of me looked exactly like what I had envisioned in my prayers all this time. I shouted, "This is a beautiful mahogany desk made from sturdy Philippine mahogany. This is a chair with wheels from Mitsubishi, and this is a strong American bicycle. Thank you, God! Everyone, look! God gave me everything that I prayed for."

The people who had not believed me all this time, and those church members and village people that treated me like I was crazy were all surprised at the things that God provided me. I told them the secret, "You must pray specifically. Tell God in detail what you want, and then have faith that you will receive it. Faith is believing that God will provide, and expecting it to happen even though you can't see it. He will do the same for you, as He did for me." This event brought about a great change in my life. Before experiencing this incident, I did not pray in detail and afterwards, my faith was growing and I prayed specifically and in detail. The Bible still witnesses this

The tent church.

statement, "Now faith is being sure of what we hope for and certain of what we do not see." (Hebrew 11:1)

There were many things we did not have in our church because we started the church with only a love for God. Our church was just a ragged old abandoned tent on a concrete slab left by the U.S. Military at the top of a hill, next to a cemetery. The neighbors who saw us could easily have mistaken us for beggars, and to anyone else who saw our church, we surely didn't look like a church that had any potential to grow. However, at least in my heart, I was certain that God would revive our church, so I never thought that our church would fail. With conviction from God that our church would grow I drew a picture of a full church, and saw it that way in my prayers. What do you think happened after that? Of course, due to the conviction from God many good things happened, but it was here on the hilltops of Daejo-dong that the amazing story of our church growth began.

Becoming a Carpenter

The tent church was built in a sesame field on the hill top next to the public cemetery. Our church functioned much like a family before we had even put up a sign or held a formal service. Lay Minister Choi, my prayer partner, had always dreamed of starting an orphanage. During the Korean War she had offered refuge to a family who came south from the border, and during the three years she sheltered them, she formed a close relationship with the mother of the family—they shared everything from soy sauce to bean paste.

One day at the Namdaemun Flea Market, near the time of her graduation from the seminary, Sister Choi saw two women. One of them was the woman who had stayed with her, and the other was the woman's sister. While they were talking, the woman's sister offered Sister Choi a gift of 11,862 square yards of land as a token of her appreciation for what Sister Choi had done for her sister and her family. Sister Choi's dream of setting up an orphanage became a reality. But her dream was short-lived, because she made a calamitous decision in handing over the deed to the land to a builder she was thinking of hiring without any hesitation or question. He kept the deed and the land, and just that swiftly her dream of building an orphanage disappeared along with the plot of land.

While praying tearfully afterwards, Sister Choi felt the empowering of the Holy Spirit who helped her realize that orphans aren't made up only of children who have lost their earthly parents, but also include those who do not know God the Father as their heavenly Father. Therefore, after deciding that she would become a spiritual mother, guiding precious young souls to Christ, she began teaching the Bible and hymns to children in her neighborhood in her mud-plastered home in Daejo-dong.

When I heard the news that Sister Choi had restarted the orphanage, I was delighted. I went to see her with the full intention of assessing her current circumstances and praying with her. When I arrived, I was surprised to find her sitting among the children and hunting for lice in their hair. Upon seeing this I said, "Lay Minister Choi, I've come to visit with you, and I thought you would be busy running an orphanage, but you are looking for lice."

She laughed and said, "Welcome. How is your health? And how is the preparation going for your studies abroad?"

Even though I was no longer certain of my plans to go abroad to study and was now fairly certain I would not go, I replied. "It's going well."

Sister Choi said, "I have no doubt that you will do well. You are always so passionate and hard working. Do you remember those days when you were a student and we were witnessing to those elderly folks at the Seoul Train Station and Pagoda Park? And do you remember when the bus driver refused to let us in because my drum was too big? So we ended up walking all the way to Pagoda Park from Seodae Gate as I beat on the drum?"

"That's right, that's right," I replied, "we were very bold and courageous, and we were not ashamed. Sister Choi, do you remember the hymns you sang so beautifully that day? They were certainly inspired by the Holy Spirit and brought some of the people to tears."

"Yes, I surely do remember that," she said, "but your message was better—the best. I was quite impressed when people sat down on the ground to listen to your message; they seemed totally unaware of the passing time."

Our reminiscing over past times and complimenting each other came to a halt as Sister Choi exclaimed, "Oh, by the way, did you hear? The rainy season is coming early this year. Perhaps we ought to build a sturdy house, and if God is willing move the church into it."

"I'm sure God would be pleased." I replied.

A short time after that chat, a carpenter, a helper and I prepared to begin construction on a new house. We drew up a blue print and then started figuring how what we had to build with—we had no blocks, no cement, and no building materials. But just in the nick of time we were informed that a local cement manufacturer owed some money to a close neighbor of Jasil Choi, and the neighbor said we could use as many blocks and as much cement as we needed, and pay back the money at a later time. I accepted this as the first sign of God's hand moving us along.

We gathered all the cement and blocks we needed, bought lumber on credit, and began construction on a plot of approximately 400 square yards. We started building the house block by block. With the help of Missionary Stantz, who was knowledgeable and skilled in electrical work, we were getting close to finishing the house, but as the completion of the building drew near I was becoming increasingly distressed over how to pay the workers, and how to pay the cost of the materials. Then one day a textile factory owner paid a visit to Jasil Choi, they had been in a close business relationship when she was running a business of her own. He had borrowed some money from her, and now that he had located her, he came to visit and pay back the money he had borrowed from her.

So we experienced God's workings for the second time. How could the factory owner come looking for Mother Choi with money that was long overdue at just the right time? I was really puzzled, but God knew when we would need the money, and had the factory owner find Sister Choi at the point of our need for the completion of the house. I was filled with joy as I praised Him, "Hallelujah, thank you, O God."

We thanked God for His sovereignty and guidance, and there was a growing sense of expectancy among us for God's great awesome plan. So with the money from the factory owner and money we got from selling Jasil Choi's Japanese-made sewing machine, we were able to pay the worker's wages and the creditors.

When we were drawing up the blueprint, we had envisioned this house having three rooms and a kitchen. Between two of the rooms, we put a sliding door instead of a wall so that we would be able to use the open space for our services. From our beginnings at the tent church to the wooden floor of the new house, our services were held in a family style setting. Soon after that, I laid aside all plans to go abroad to study, and moved to Lay Minister Choi's place and began full-time ministry.

The Dream Team of the Tent Church

I believe that Lay Minister Choi was a partner given to me by God. I met Lay Minister Choi, whom I called Lay Minister Mother, during my time in seminary when I was the student body president and she was in charge of evangelism in the seminary. During those times, the aftermath of tuberculosis had me sick quite frequently. I was always sick with a cold, and every time I was sick, Lay Minister Choi, whose former occupation was a nurse, would nurse me back to health and pray for me as if I was one of her children. Thus we got even closer. When I asked her if I could call her "Mother" our conversation went like this: "Sister Choi."

"Yes, what is it, student president Cho?" she asked.

"Well, I would like to call you 'Mother' from now on," I said. "You're always praying for me, and taking care of me when I get sick. I would like to call you 'Mother' because you take care of me like a mother. Would that be all right with you?" She looked at me with her smiling eyes and lovingly nodded yes. Since that time, I have been calling Lay Minister Choi "Mother."

I believe God brought us to each other as a dream team to do His work. In the church, Lay Minister Choi was known as the problem solver, because she listened to and helped solve the various problems of the people, and I was the preacher who touched people with God's Word, and helped them accept Jesus. To whoever saw us, it was apparent that we were perfect partners in the tent church brought together by God. Even more so, we were friends from heaven that prayed in harmony.

Since we had no members to minister to in the beginning, we both got up at 4:30 in the morning and prayed together until seven, then after having breakfast we prayed again until noon. After a short rest, we prayed together until the evening. God allowed us to be partners and guided us to pray to Him daily for ten hours, because He was teaching us how to start His church and how to pray to Him.

Through this training, we prayed without stopping, even if at times we could not put food on the table. These times of deep prayer enabled us to have pity on the village people and pray for them. "God! Please help these people. Please lead them to have faith in you and deliver them from poverty, disease, and evil. Let many people come to church to hear your Words and learn about the gospel. Praise you O Lord!" We really must have prayed at the top of our lungs because, according to some, they were able to hear our prayers all the way to the bus station, which was quite a ways from the church. This daily prayer guided by the Holy Spirit to help the village people experience Jesus' salvation was gradually starting to accumulate in the prayer storage box of Heaven.

Looking with Eyes of Faith and Rules of Church Growth

In May, the start of that year's long summer, Lay Minister Jasil Choi and I went to every corner of the village to witness to each and every home. Walking through the village we called out, "Come hear our good news about God and His Son, Jesus! Hear about Jesus and believe in Him, then you will be saved! Jesus will save you and cure your of your diseases and provide for all your needs!" Seeing an elderly Grandpa, we called out to him, "Grandpa! You should believe in Jesus, too!"

"If I believe in Jesus, will He give me the rice wine that I like so much for free?" he asked.

"Of course!" we answered, "and God will give you something even better! So come to church and hear about Jesus."

However, the village people who heard our message gave us a chilly response. They didn't believe the gospel we were preaching, so, naturally, they disregarded what we said. The people even told others not to believe us and accused us of lying. But every time that happened, God consoled us, *"Do not be disappointed that no one is listening. I am always by your side."*

A month had passed since the church officially opened. The size of the congregation grew quite large. The local lady shamans threatened us and began spreading rumors that attending church would lead to ruin and even bankruptcy. One day in June, I heard of a woman who had been suffering from paralysis for seven years. She was known as "Musung's mom"—it was common to refer to mothers by their son's first name. Right after delivering her son, she had become paralyzed and had not gotten up since.

During my years in seminary, I had heard from missionaries about the healing power of the Holy Spirit and God's awesome workings. In the subsequent years, when I began working with the missionaries, I saw with my own two eyes the evidence of His power. Also, my eyes were opened by reading books on the spiritual warfare of the great evangelists of the past. Most importantly, I was led to the thought of healing her through prayer while reading the many passages where Jesus healed the multitudes during His ministry.

Musung's mom lived in an area quite a distance from the church. When we arrived at her home, which was more like a hut and leaned so much it looked like the leaning Tower of Pisa, we heard a baby crying feebly. I carefully pulled the sliding doors to one side. The day was quite sunny and pleasant, typical of spring, but inside the room was quite dark. Lying on some thick, dirty, blankets was a pale-looking mother and a newborn. In appearance, the mother was nothing but bones and leathery skin; next to her was a baby with an undersized body and an unusually large head. Instantly, my heart was overcome with emotion but the rest of me was bowled over by the stench. It didn't take long for me to discover what was causing the terrible smell. Musung's mom had been bedridden for seven years without much assistance or care, not even with bowel movements. On top of that, she had given birth to a child; both were a terrible mess. Lay Minister Choi bathed them immediately. While she was washing them we sang hymns loudly.

What can wash away my sin?
Nothing but the blood of Jesus;
What can make me whole again?
Nothing but the blood of Jesus.

We thought we were poor but their situation was far worse. Lay Minister Choi and I firmly grabbed Musung's mom's hands and prayed in tears. "Heavenly Father, we lift up Musung's mom. Heal her paralysis. You, who healed a man with paralysis for thirty-eight years, have compassion on this soul." Then

33

we spoke to the evil spirit of paralysis, "You evil spirit! We command you in the name of Jesus to release your stronghold on this woman."

The setting of the sun to the west indicated that some time had passed, so we left to go home. At home, we ate corn porridge for supper, and that evening began our prayers interceding for Musung's mom. We prayed late into the night. Early the next morning we paid them another visit. We repeated the same procedure on the third day.

On the morning of the fourth day, I was greeted with great news from her husband, "She no longer says anything negative or has self pity," he said. "Instead, she now has the will to live, and to carry on." That was certainly delightful news to our ears. We went to visit her, and when we arrived at her home, she said, "Why should I end my life?"

We encouraged her and said, "Jesus was flogged for our illnesses and was crucified on the Cross. Do not worry; just place your faith in Him, Musung's mom, and you will surely rise to your feet." Sister Choi and I laid our hands on her, prayed in tongues, and strongly commanded away the evil spirits. "We command in the name of Jesus Christ, be healed from paralysis. We command in the name of Jesus Christ, depart from her, you evil spirits."

Both of us were soaked in sweat and our voices turned raspy. We must have prayed for several hours—then a miracle occurred. Musing's mom yelled at the top of her lungs, "Jesus! Hallelujah! I feel refreshed, and really invigorated!" We opened our eyes and gazed at her face. To our amazement, against what seemed like big drops of sweat dripping, her face glowed as if the sun was shining on it.

We quickly turned to James 4:7, "Submit yourselves therefore to God. Resist the devil, and he will flee from you." With that verse, we boldly continued casting out evil spirits. "You evil spirits of paralysis! You evil spirits who bring pains and poverty, we command in the name of Jesus Christ, release her from your bondage. Depart from her at once!" The room was filled with God's love and the powerful presence of the Holy Spirit. Musing's mom's body began to shake and great drops of sweat dripped from her as we continued our bold prayers and commanding the evil spirits away—amazingly, the baby slept peacefully through all the loud noise we were making.

After we prayed, Musung's mom tried to get up by raising the upper half of her body on her own. Because she had been bedridden for many years, even that trivial movement required a great effort from her bony body. We simply watched in amazement, wondering where such courageous strength sprang from. After each try, she fell to her buttocks, but that alone was a miracle in itself. Her husband sat in one corner of the room with his jaw dropping to the floor. "Jesus, thank you. God, thank you," she shouted, impelled by a strong sense of gratitude. We sat her against a wall and wiped away her sweat. Sister Choi asked what had compelled her to try to get up.

She replied, "While you were praying for me I felt a cool breeze, the kind of breeze that blows through the pine groves, and at that moment, the numbness and the burning sensation disappeared and out came this shout. Thank you, thank you. I grew up without my mom or siblings." Then tears ran down her cheeks as she hugged Sister Choi, who held her tenderly as they cried together. I had to lift up another prayer for her, so I laid both of my hands on her head and started praying. Right at that moment, she began to pray in tongues fluently. We took that as a sign of her being filled with the Holy Spirit. So once again I commanded with the authority of Jesus Christ.

"I rebuke all remaining evil spirits from this body." Then I told her, "You shall be healed and you shall rise!"

A miracle unfolded before our very eyes. Musung's mom pushed herself up against the wall and got up on her own two feet. Then slowly she began to take small steps. "Hallelujah!" she cried. "Thank you, God!" Then we all cried out, " She's walking. Musung's mom is walking! God is alive!" We praised God and thanked Him. Musung's mom landed on her bottom several times but she kept getting up again—she didn't give up. Her hardened body of seven years was moving as she became a new being. Soon after, she was completely cured from the paralysis, and with a healthy body she started attending the tent church. Just like that, another member joined our church family.

The day Musung's mom came to attend the church service with her hair neatly combed into place, she became the talk of the town. A patient on her deathbed was now up and walking around with a healthy complexion. The local female shamans were frightened when they heard what had happened.

Reliving the Great Revival of Pyongyang

After witnessing the miracle of Musung's mom, people in the town began to show interest in the church. Apparently a rumor was spreading that there was something mysterious inside the church and that the local female shamans were frightened, which piqued people's curiosity even more. One of the first to show a reaction was an old woman shaman. She had regularly performed two exorcisms a year, so she was quite distraught about losing her "customers" and the spirits she relied on for her powers.

What God was doing reminded us of the apostolic churches. The local shamans and fortune-tellers repented of their sins, burned all their articles of spirit worship and accepted Christ.

36

Alcoholics and patients with tuberculosis received healings. The church was becoming a prayer mountain, where people came looking for grace and zealous for healings.

One Sunday morning, Lay Minister Choi witnessed to a local woman who lived in a hut and brought the rather shabbily dressed woman to church. That day I was preaching from the passage in Mark 9:43-49. "It's better to go to heaven with one arm than to go to hell with two. Do you have any idea how scary hell is? People commit suicide more often nowadays; it has become very common, but all of them are going to hell."

During the preaching of the message, I caught a glimpse of the lady and saw her eyes filled with tears. By the help of the Holy Spirit the sermon that day was unusually full of grace, even to my ears. When it was time to pray out loud, people prayed earnestly for some time. After the prayer, I made an altar call. Knowing how important it was for people to acknowledge the lordship of Christ, I never left it out of the order of the service. As I gave the altar call I said, "Jesus is calling out to you once again. If you've decided to accept Christ as your Lord and Savior, please stand up where you are. We don't know the hour or the place when He will summon our spirits home. Please stand up, and I'll pray on your behalf." The lady stood up, her hands covering her face, which was bathed in tears, and recited the prayer of salvation after me. "I still don't know who Jesus is or what He does," she said. "But I was told to come to church, so I did, and I don't know why I'm sobbing so much."

During the time of sharing testimony, she told her story: "Over a week ago we ran out of food at our house, so we were just planning to end our lives. I have two sons, but I thought it would be too hard to convince the older one, so I took my four-year old and some rat poison and went up to the gorge in Nokbon. I planned to feed him some and then eat the rest myself. But he kept resisting it saying, 'No, I won't die. I don't want to die!' I kept trying to get him to eat it, but all of sudden, I felt something pull me by the nape of my neck. It was my husband. That was how we survived.

"Then yesterday I decided to kill myself again, but I didn't want to die and leave behind all the dirty laundry, so I took it down to an open ditch and washed the clothes. That was when that lady (pointing to Lay Minister Choi) came up to me and said, 'You look like you just want to end it all here.' She sounded as if she knew what I was going through. She was right. That morning, I had put some rat poison in my pocket. Now this morning I found myself coming to the church, and after hearing your message my heart felt liberated, and for no reason I just started crying endlessly. I no longer have any desire to end my life, and I don't know who Jesus is right now, but I believe in Him."

Once her testimony ended, there were loud shouts of "Halleluiah!" resonating throughout the church. I cried and Sister Choi did too. The testimony of the converted suicidal lady served as a turning point for the entire congregation. I felt as if all of my hard labor was paying off.

Some time passed and the woman came to church faithfully, and brought her husband to church as well. Apparently she made several threatening notices to him that she would commit suicide if he didn't come with her. The husband was saved and filled with the Holy Spirit, and came to church faithfully for some time. He even started a business and through God's blessings began to tithe faithfully—he also became a deacon. Then one night during an all-night service, I was moved by the Holy Spirit to get up and say: *"Philip Park! Why are you stealing from my tithe! The tithe is not yours. I shall close down your business!"*

I looked over at Deacon Park and his wife. Thankfully, they were bowing low, weeping and repenting in tears. The Holy Spirit was moving in their hearts. Once again, I prayed in tongues and interpreted the prayer. *"My beloved son and daughter, look unto me. The hardship and poverty in this tent church will not last forever. Look! I shall place you under my silver wings and you shall witness the gospel to the ends of the earth."*

At that moment, I was empowered by the Holy Spirit and began singing a worship hymn with Sister Choi. It was truly a blessed moment, filled with the Spirit of God. Everyone there that evening was filled with the Holy Spirit and reverently received the prophetic words of God coming out of my mouth. Our circumstances were quite dire but I felt as if I was living in some moment in the future.

Some time passed after the Holy Spirit had me rebuke Deacon Park, and eventually Deacon Park had to close down his sawdust manufacturing company. He shared this testimony at church one morning, "We had been tithing for five months straight, and the amount we tithed became too valuable to me, so I suggested to my wife that we could earn a large sum of money by entering a local lottery scheme, then the amount we could tithe would increase and be of more significance for support of the church. I thought the reason was well justified since we were doing it all for God. Little did I know this was not His way, and that night when God used Lay Minister Cho to rebuke us, we repented. So we are not disappointed at all in God for closing down the company. I have faith that God will return it to us someday."

When Deacon Park finished speaking, a spirit of repentance began to flow through the congregation, even some local hooligans repented of their sins and accepted Christ. A few from the group even committed their lives to become His servants. It was like the great 1907 revival of Pyongyang.

On January 14, 1907, a group of Korean Christians and Western missionaries met in Pyongyang for a Bible study in the Changdaehyun Church on the outskirts of the city. Halfway through the Bible study, God began to move. One after another, the Christians confessed their sins as they were impelled to their feet, tears of repentance streaming down their faces. The wave of repentance continued the next day, and soon conviction of sins and repentance spread throughout the city as the Holy Spirit moved in great convicting power. From there it spread throughout Korea, resulting in a revival that lasted for forty years, brought thousands into the Kingdom, and established hundreds of Christian churches across the nation.

A Hole in the Tent Church

Church members longing for His grace practically lived at the church. They even dug a hole on a hill and turned it into a furnace to cook rice. They ate and slept at the church, all of them joyously sought the grace of the Holy Spirit. In the winter, they spread straw bags over the frozen concrete floor to pray until one or two in the morning, then they would nap for a few hours and be up at four in the morning for early-morning

The tent church in Daejo-dong.

prayer services. During the day, they went out to Daejo-dong and witnessed to people, beating on a drum to attract crowds. It was a difficult and hard time for everyone, but they were filled with peace and joy. Soon the congregation grew and multiplied by the work of the Holy Spirit, and we saw a need for a bigger church.

A year had passed since we started services at Choi's home. Now, it was filled with people and patients from all walks of life and no longer could contain the multitude. So Lay Minister Choi and I decided to raise up a tent church in front of the house.

During those financially difficult times, some of Choi's valuable personal ornaments came in handy. We sold a pear-shaped gold ornament to buy some tent materials at the Dongdaemun Flea Market. We unfolded the tent to discover a large hole, so it posed a problem on rainy days. Although we were disappointed, we thanked God for even allowing us to have such a precious tent. With some straw bags covering the ground, it didn't look too shabby.

There on the wooden floor of Choi's home with a few members, the core membership of what would become the Yoido Full Gospel Church began. After we set up the tent church in her front yard, we experienced a rapid growth in number and size. The Holy Spirit moved powerfully through the church. Ultimately, the tent church became the very symbol of God's presence and a revival in the pioneering days of the church.

A Disabled Boy Walks
One day, a crippled shoeshine boy working at the Seoul Train Station came to the tent church. He had heard from someone that he might get his legs fixed if he just came to the church. In spite of the cruel treatment and teasing he received from

the bus driver he got on the bus, and in faith came to church for a healing.

It was only October but it felt like winter had already started. The cold wind bit into our skin and the raindrops fell like tips of icicles. The straw mats were like ice on the frozen ground. But despite the weather conditions, the tent church was filled with a large crowd, and sitting there among them that evening was the disabled boy. I passionately proclaimed a message of hope from the pulpit, sweating even in that freezing temperature. "Our God is a good father. Our circumstances may seem bleak but if we stand firmly rooted in Jesus by faith. Some day His blessings shall come upon us, and our very flesh, spirit, and lifestyle will undergo a change. Have hope in Jesus, for He is our hope. If you are ill, have hope in Him for your healing; if you are in poverty, have hope in Him to provide for all your needs through the glorious riches that are in Christ Jesus."

After the service, the disabled boy came to me asking for a prayer. "Lay Minister Cho, I want to walk again," he said. "Please help me."

"Do you really believe you can walk again?" I asked.

"I do," he replied. "If you will pray for me, I have faith in God that He will heal me."

Looking into his eyes, I could see how serious he was, so I earnestly started praying for him. I prayed for him as if I was the one in pain. The congregation joined me, and prayed earnestly for the boy. Some time passed, then I reached out and grabbed his arm and pulled him up in faith. But there was no response in the boy's physical condition. We started praying again, and once again nothing took place in his shriveled legs. So I eagerly waited for God to respond to our prayers. I had to. Then I prayed again. "Oh God, have compassion on this boy's soul. If you won't fix him, I won't continue my ministry here. Have pity on me, Oh Father."

I put my heart and soul into my prayers, and for some unknown reason, I felt deeply attached to the boy and my heart really went out to him. I opened my eyes and pulled him up again with all my strength and yelled out, "In the name of Jesus Christ, I command these legs to straighten out! In the name of Jesus Christ, I command this disabled boy shall get up! Get up!"

A few moments later there was a loud shout of joy inside the church. The disabled boy got up and started walking. All the members of the congregation jumped up and down rejoicing, clapping their hands, and praising God. I too became overwhelmed and thanked and praised Him. "Our living God, thank you. You've used this weak servant as your tool. I return all the glory to you. I hope and pray that you, Oh God, will use this church to carry out your grand plan."

The boy took small steps at first and then started running. His life had just taken on new meaning. And through that miracle the church experienced yet another growth explosion. People told of what happened and the stories spread by word of mouth throughout the region, causing people from far distances to come and bring their loved ones with physical disabilities. All these were miraculous signs done by God to us who believed in Him and looked upon Him with hope and faith.

Poor Neighborhood, Needy Church

People with all types of illnesses—stroke, stomach disorder, rheumatism, tuberculosis, physical disability—came and received healing from the Holy Spirit. Even the local hooligans and troublemakers had a change of heart and became members of the congregation. However, the church was always in financial difficulty. Daejo-dong was a ghetto and most people living there were either sick or poor, and the others who came to this town came after their businesses failed or after filing bankruptcy. Therefore, the offering was often sparse because the people had no money.

The average amount we collected per week was 200 hwan. (approximately $2.00 in U.S. currency). With that amount, the church was unable to carry out even its most basic functions. It wasn't sufficient to even pay for gasoline. So we really couldn't do anything about the pressures of dealing with necessities of life. All three meals were pretty much the same—corn porridge with salty radishes as a side dish. At rare times we had soup made with bean sprouts; it was considered a feast. To live we had to eat, and being able to eat meant we were living.

From the 3000 hwan I earned interpreting for missionaries at the seminary, I used 500 hwan for the roundtrip transportation fee and 300 hwan for tithing. All I had left to survive on was 2200 hwan. I gave the rest of the money to Lay Minister Choi to buy corn powder for the porridge and briquettes to keep the rooms warm. There was nothing left at that point. So Choi's daughter, Sunghye, who attended Seoul Girl's High School, gave private piano lessons late into the night and earned roughly 3000 hwan. Along with this supplemental income, Choi would occasionally sell her personal belongings, such as rings and other valuables, to get money to survive.

Sunghye became the church pianist when an American soldier donated an old Yamaha piano to the church. She played for all services, including the early morning prayer services. She would wake up at 4:30 A.M., play at the service and then leave for school. As a result, she was frequently sleep-deprived, but she knew she had to continue to give her private piano lessons. We had pity on her, but there was nothing we could do except continue to encourage her, for the money was necessary. In order to survive, everyone had to contribute.

Wearing Pajamas and Bare Feet

Even with my poor health, I had to rely on the bus to travel, which was always loaded with passengers. I would return home exhausted from having to interpret all day. On top of that, I led the Wednesday night service and all-night prayer service. When delivering God's message I gave my all, and I would also pray in tongues and do the laying on of hands, which required much strength and effort on my part. So after the service I often felt jittery and dizzy and could not sleep. In spite of the severe sleep deprivation, I was up on my feet at 4:00 A.M. to lead the early morning prayer service.

Lay Minister Choi made home visits during the day, and attended all of the all-night services, and always prayed for others by the laying on of hands. She, too, woke up 4:00 A.M. to attend the early morning prayer service, and at times she even fasted.

What made things worse was that we had to sleep in cold rooms on a blanket on the floor and a thin blanket to cover us to create some sort of warmth. Falling asleep is quite challenging with an empty growling stomach, but usually around 2:00 A.M. we would fall asleep with our thin blankets wrapped around our bodies trying to generate enough body heat to warm us. Sometimes having to wake up again in two hours was worse than having to go to sleep—there were times it was almost unbearable.

One night I was sound asleep when Lay Minister Choi walked in with a water basin full of water. "Lay minister Cho," she said, "I brought some water and a towel. It's time to lead the service."

"Oh no, leave me alone!" I said. "How can a human being live under such conditions? Do you have any idea how much sleep I've had? Two hours! I have only slept the last two hours. Who started these early morning prayer services anyway?" I was so tired, I was irritable and foolish.

One early morning I woke up, but I was so tired that I really couldn't tell if I was still sleeping and dreaming or wide awake. I put on my clothes automatically, piece by piece. As I walked into the church, people looked at me strangely and whispered to one another, but no one voiced any concerns and the service went rather nicely. As I left the chapel, I discovered what the strange looks and whispering had been about. I saw my reflection in a window—I had managed to put on a shirt and a tie and jacket, but my lower garments consisted of pajamas and no socks. I was so embarrassed that I ran out like a 100-meter sprinter. Lack of sleep, poor nutrition, and fatigue had all culminated into a forgetful and somewhat shameful act. However, the church members graciously forgave me and had pity on me. They came to the conclusion that I really must have been tired to do such a thing.

A Humorous Maggot Incident

At times, even managing two meals a day was difficult. Lunch was usually a time for fasting, but there were times we would skip breakfast and dinner as well. Before this time, I would often turn down even some of the gourmet dishes, but nowadays something as simple and basic as soup prepared with dried radish leaves in bean paste with barley wheat rice was a feast from heaven. There were many days when we didn't even have that. Having such hunger in my life, I sympathized with the other members of the congregation and took to heart what they might be going through on a daily basis.

Lay Minister Choi was always concerned for my health and felt she wasn't doing enough to care for me. To see someone like me, who was young and had a bright future ahead, suffering in these conditions was difficult for her to bear. Since she was already advanced in age, she didn't care how her life would turn out; but seeing me doing ministry work with the poor and the sick, and with financial difficulties to boot, she couldn't help but feel sorry for me. She once mentioned that she even carried a guilty conscience about preventing me from going abroad to study and forcing me to spend my youthful days in vain.

One day after making home visits, Lay minister Choi returned home with various sorts of wild greens, some green onions, bean paste, and a jar of salted shrimp used for seasoning. We knew we were in for a real treat; our mouths watered as she prepared the tasty, savory bean paste soup. I started to eat, and then quickly stopped. "Yuck, what is this?" I said. "Oh, Lord Jesus!" I caught a glimpse of Sister Choi from the corner of my eye, and as I stared down into the soup bowl I said, "Hey, you! I suppose you belong in the protein category but I wonder if I should spare your life and toss you out or just chew you up. You know what, I'm going to spare your life today. Be gone!"

We later found out that she had bought the bean paste and jar of salted shrimp from a close acquaintance, but when she brought it home she was shocked to discover swarming maggots underneath the top layer of salted shrimp. Somehow she managed to pick them out one by one and continued to prepare supper that night, which everyone was eagerly awaiting. She had reluctantly used the salted shrimp to make the bean paste soup. But she hadn't found all of the maggots, there was one left and it ended up in my bowl, much to Sister Choi's embarrassment. Realizing her warm intentions to care for me with love and devotion, I embraced her attempts to take care of me with the utmost respect and gratitude. In an effort to lighten the mood, I humorously tried to make light of this incident. She quickly ran out of the room trying to hide her tears. During those days Sister Choi often recalled the glorious times when she had lived comfortably and never had to worry about such trivial matters, like having enough to eat, or what was in the food.

Regret Over Losing a Lottery

There was a strange rumor going around that someone had purchased the surrounding land where the church was built and wanted to tear down the church. It was absurd. I quickly went over to the church to find Sister Choi. "Lay Minister Choi," I said, "we need to talk."

"Why, is everything all right?" she asked.

"We have a serious problem," I replied. "Someone purchased the land around the church and wants us to vacate immediately. They want to tear down the church."

"Why would they want to do that?" she asked.

"Well," I replied, "apparently some people consider the healings that take place at the church as heresy."

"If the healing miracles are considered heresy," she said, "doesn't that make Jesus a heretic?"

I sensed that something terrible was on the verge of unfolding. I believed it was persecution, a spiritual battle, a war. Sister Choi and I fell on our knees before God; we had no choice but to cling to Him again. We had no time to belabor the situation. We began fasting and prayed earnestly and tearfully.

Soon after, an old lady who had been healed from a stomach disorder came to find out what the fuss was about. Sister Choi confided in the woman, and shared the details, thinking she seemed like a motherly figure. Two days later, the lady returned with her two sons who offered to build an elevated bridge and overpass for the church, so people could get to church by crossing the surrounding land. We thought it would be impractical to have a bridge since there were too many people with serious illnesses coming to church, which would make it difficult for them to get around. So we kindly turned down the offer.

A few days later, I saw an ad in the local newspaper. The ad was for a lottery and it listed the first place prize as an apartment and the second place prize as a brand new car. Considering this new crisis and our measly church budget, I felt a strong pull toward taking this gamble but had some qualms about utilizing worldly ways to help the church. Lay Minister Choi must have been thinking the same thing.

"Lay Minister Cho, there is this ad in the newspaper about a lottery," she said. "As long as we don't indulge in it for selfish desires, perhaps God might bless our intentions." I told her I wasn't certain that servants of God should buy lottery tickets, and she replied, "Why not? God might be offering it to us, you never know. After all, God used ravens to feed Elijah."

That convinced me, but the cost of a ticket was two hundred hwan and I only had twenty hwan. "Do you have that much money Sister Choi?" I asked. She just looked at me and shook her head.

So that evening, we borrowed 400 hwan from a neighbor and bought two tickets. The day of the lottery finally arrived, and prepared for anything we packed a sack lunch and went to Capitol Plaza where the lottery drawing was to take place.

We were praying in tongues on the train, clapping our hands, and yelling out, "We believe!" We did not care whether people were staring at us—desperate times required desperate measures. The fate of the church rested on this day, so we fully embraced this adventure.

We arrived at the plaza and walked into the midst of a swarming crowd. People were already lined up and waiting for the event to start. We prayed and waited with the others. It was a scorching-hot day, and at times we felt dizzy from the heat as we stood in the burning sun.

Finally, it was our turn. Lay Minister Choi went first to draw the winning number. She stuck her hand up to her forearm into a big barrel full of what looked like tickets. She rummaged through the pile several times, and with her eyes closed pulled her arm out of the barrel with a ticket held firmly in her hand—she was probably praying in tongues up to the minute she pulled that ticket out. Then she looked down at the piece of paper in her hand, it was blank—not the winning ticket. I watched her closely as her face that had been so full of expectation fell with disappointment.

"Stand aside," I said, "you have to place fifth at least to take home a prize like soap or something." I gave her a little nudge and chuckled as I walked past her. I took in a deep breath and yelled out "Lord!" just loud enough for the person next to me to hear. I reached into the barrel and grabbed a ticket—I couldn't believe my eyes, it too was blank, a dud.

"You see, you didn't get anything either." Sister Choi said chidingly.

"Let's go now," I replied. "What did I tell you? God's servants shouldn't be taking part in a lottery."

I was deeply embarrassed and disappointed as I took long strides and passed Lay Minister Choi. I wanted to maintain some distance between us because she was crying. She just trailed behind me dragging her feet as her shadow crisscrossed mine in the afternoon sun. I was feeling upset over the whole thing also, and I thought I should say something to her. "Why are you crying?" I said. "You're attracting attention. I'm sure God has another plan for us." But I was very uncertain now.

We got back on the train and sat apart from each other. Both of us were disappointed and regretted taking such a chance on a risky opportunity. I prayed on our way back to the church, but I'm sure I sounded like a grumbling child let down because things didn't go his way. "God, I can't carry on the ministry any longer," I grumbled. "This is getting too difficult. The church doesn't have any money. How am I going to expand the tent church? I'm getting burnt out, God. I can't go on this way much longer." Right then something strange occurred. God responded immediately to this querulous child of His—talk about and instant answer to prayer! As the train was passing by a theater near Seodae Gate, the Holy Spirit spoke to my heart. *"Do you see that theater?"*

"I do, Lord." I said.

"How many stories are there?" the Holy Spirit asked.

"Two stories." I replied.

"I shall give you a church bigger than that theater. Do you believe it?" He asked.

"Yes, I do." I responded. "I believe it, Lord." I couldn't figure out what had just happened, but hearing that inner voice made me realize that I had been wrong to grumble about not carrying on the ministry. I repented immediately. Then I elbowed my way through the passengers to where Lay Minister Choi was seated and told her what had happened. I urged her to accept God's will for our ministry by saying "Amen."

Lay Minister Choi almost shouted, "Amen!"

From that point on, we prayed feverishly night and day, believing that God would grant us a building—a church larger than the theater. It was a very difficult time for all of us, so difficult in fact that I had resorted to playing the lottery and justified it as the right thing to do. I was mistaken; prayer was the only answer. We had to pray! The only way to protect the church from the attacks of the devil was by prayer, and pray we did. God moved quickly, and it wasn't long before He began to solve our problems.

Enlistment Notice

A red envelope arrived with the biting, piercing, north wind on the morning of January 3, 1961. While shoveling snow in the front yard, Lay Minister Choi received the notice and brought it in. It was an enlistment notice, and it was addressed to me. While in seminary, I had received a physical exam to serve in the military but was rejected due to physical illness; I was no longer ill, but now after I read the notice, I said, "Well, if I can't serve in the military, what good am I? I'm a man; it's my duty and privilege to serve my country." But even as I carried out my bravado, I couldn't help but worry about the church.

Staring at the dark clouds overhead, Sister Choi said softly, "What are we going to do now?"

Just when we were able to take a leap to a new level of growth for the church, I was faced with this unwelcome summons. With sweat and tears as fertilizer to cultivate the church from what it was three years ago, we had grown the congregation to

A very young Dr. Cho.

four hundred members. A deacon who received healing from a serious heart condition had made a handsome offering and we were able to purchase 2400 square yards of land, and we had even developed plans to build a new church in the spring. Staring at the enlistment notice, I thought, "With everything going right, suddenly things are falling apart again and becoming a shambles." To make matters worse, I had less than three weeks until I had to check in at the base.

My mind went blank with the thought of leaving the church for three years. Lay Minister Choi was upfront about how she felt. "I can pray night and day, even fast for ten to fifteen days," she said, "but to be left in charge, Lay Minister Cho, I can't do it by myself."

I feared that the congregation would become greatly distressed over the news, so I decided not to say anything until I had actually found a replacement pastor. But finding a replacement wasn't easy. I sought out a number of missionaries I knew, but none of them could take over my post at the church. With no solid leads and my options running out, I just announced the news to the congregation and asked for their prayers. The entire congregation fasted and prayed earnestly, desperately.

It was two or three days before my time to leave, when Missionary J.W. Hurston paid an unexpected visit from Busan. He greeted us warmly, and then told us that the Holy Spirit kept inspiring him during his prayers to come to our tent church. So we told him everything, and without hesitation, he agreed to lead the church.

January 30, the day I was to report to boot camp, finally arrived. Snowflakes fluttered and blew around intensely as the north wind unleashed its force. The night before, the only briquette left had gone out, so when I left the house early the next morning, I had no warm water to thaw my frigid body. Thankfully, Sister Choi had sent her children out earlier to pick up some bread and milk for me to take on my trip.

I arrived later that day at the boot camp in Nohnsan city. Upon arrival, I received another physical. I passed. Some time later, I wrote to the congregation, for my mind was constantly preoccupied with the church, both before and during hard trainings. Toward the end of February, Lay Minister Choi and several members of the women's group paid me a visit. They brought with them a whole cooked chicken and some soup made with rice cakes and vegetables. "Lay Minister Cho," they said, "we're here to visit you."

"Hallelujah," I said happily, "it's good to see you. How are things going at the church?" My first words were about the church because it was the only thing I could think about, it was on my mind constantly. Some of the soldiers from my barracks gladly joined us to share the food. Lay Minister Choi began crying as soon as she saw me, because I looked so different.

I had lost more weight because of the intense training, and the cold weather had toughened up my skin. She wouldn't stop crying. "Are you okay?" She asked with a concerned voice. "How is your health?"

"I'm fine." I said. "I'm even better now that you have come to see me. Calm down. Look, I'm really okay." To impress her, I saluted her in military fashion. From that visit on until I was relocated to a base, church members came to visit me weekly, bringing food and comfort. I was deeply grateful.

On March 15, by God's grace, I was assigned to a base close to Seoul. Thankfully, due to the location of the base, I could now go to church for Sunday service and help out wherever I was needed. Easter Sunday was just around the corner, and I thought it would be good to have a baptismal Sunday service. Lay Minister Choi pleaded with me to wait until I had some time to recuperate and the weather warmed up, but I stubbornly argued that having the baptism would be more significant before Easter. So, I made the announcement that Sunday.

At the Threshold of Death

The first Sunday service of April, we conducted the baptism along with pre-baptism confession. The weather was quite chilly from a spring rain the day before. Susaek River, where we planned to have the full submersion baptism ceremony, was still cold enough to freeze your hands. Those who were being baptized didn't have to worry about it since after the submersion they could quickly change into their dry clothes and warm up next to a bonfire. But missionary Hurston and I had to remain in the water, chest high, for nearly two hours.

Baptism service in the river near the tent church in Daejo-dong.

My body shivered and my lips turned blue. I was in the water in my soldier uniform without any additional clothing. Lay Minister Choi seemed terribly concerned about my condition. But it was a joyous time—the congregation rejoiced, praised God, and sang hymns. Thankfully the ceremony ended without any mishap.

That evening I had to return to the base even before my clothes could dry. I got to the base, but during the night something inside of me ruptured, and I was taken to the emergency room on the base. I was later told that my surgery which started at eight in the morning didn't end until after four in the afternoon. In addition to the rupture, while in the hospital I quickly developed pneumonia, and they put me into the critical care ward. I was semiconscious and could hardly raise my head, but I heard someone call out my name, "Lay Minister Cho." It was some of the church members and Lay Minister Choi. I said to them softly, "The gospel is spread only through sacrifice."

"Oh, Lord!" Lay Minister Choi cried out while firmly grabbing my hands. I could barely keep my eyes open. She wept bitterly with her eyes fixed on me. She had come to the hospital to stay and care for me, while the congregation prayed and interceded for my health. The pain was excruciating, and I was drenched in sweat as I moaned and groaned in an effort to lessen the pain. Lay Minister Choi wiped off my sweat and changed my wet clothes with some extra clothes she had brought. The pain left me no room to feel embarrassed or uncomfortable about being changed or seen naked by Lay Minister Choi. She hand washed my clothes and hung them to dry by the windowsill. She then came back to my bed, knelt on the floor, and prayed.

Later that evening, Missionary Hurston came to visit. In despair, I blurted out my thoughts. "Reverend Hurston, I think God is going to take me to heaven."

"No, no," he said, "you still have much to do here, Brother Cho. God is not going to call you home yet."

Reverend Hurston tearfully and earnestly prayed for me, and from that evening on the congregation held an all-night service every night at the tent church. Many church members came to visit, and seeing them made me very happy and encouraged. By my second night in the ward, however, my temperature rose to 40° Celsius (104° Fahrenheit), and I tried desperately to ride out the waves of pain assaulting my body. That night ten of the patients in the hospital died and were taken down to the in-house mortuary.

A few days later, the doctor called in Lay Minister Choi, as my next of kin, and announced that my condition was incurable. "The patient is suffering from serious after effects," he said, "and every time he has spasms of coughing the stitched areas burst open again. He is not healing as I had hoped he would. If he doesn't start getting better soon, you ought to start preparing for what's to come."

My temperature rose constantly and my coughing turned quite severe. At times, I was in a state of unconsciousness and was often delirious. I was at the threshold of death. Unfailingly, Lay Minister Choi continued to pray—earnestly and passionately, and because the room was so small, she had to crawl underneath my hospital bed. She prayed, "God, protect your son. Please stop his coughing, right now. Your beloved servant, Pastor Cho, got sick while conducting baptisms to commemorate the death of your Son. Lord! Lord! Lord! Carry out your will to prove that his work wasn't done in vain."

I lay there listening to her fervent prayers—I was so sick I couldn't sleep. "Mother, stop praying," I said. "I think God is done with me now."

"Don't say that!" she said. "God isn't through with you yet. You were called for His purpose, and you still have work to do." Lay Minister Choi left the room. She later said she didn't want me to hear her crying and would go somewhere else to pray. She was convinced that there was no other option but to cling to God. She was desperate for an answer. She went outside to a tall, straight, boulder buried in the middle of the hospital garden and prayed with great intensity and feeling.

"Oh God, as you know, our church members have experienced your awesome and powerful healings. The disabled get up, walk and run! You healed patients from stroke and tuberculosis. But, look at your servant, Pastor Cho; he is at the brink of death. Why have you not healed him? What if he dies? What is going to happen to your church? We have been called heretics because of your miraculous healings, your very own works. If he dies we won't be able to witness any longer, then the church members will be scattered in all directions. The church falling apart, Pastor Cho dying—what will I do with myself?"

As Lay Minister Choi conversed with God, I had a dream. A big yellow serpent appeared out of nowhere and entangled my body in an attempt to kill me. Then a thick, dense, smoke began to rise and soon it engulfed me and the serpent—and in the smoke the serpent died. I woke up, drenched in sweat, to see Lay Minister Choi carefully wiping the sweat away from my face. I called out her name with all the strength I had. "Lay Minister Choi, Mother, I am going to be okay now. I'm alive, and I feel so refreshed." I told her about the dream as she cried tears of joy. "Amen. Hallelujah!" I exclaimed. "Our living God has spared my life!"

Sister Choi said excitedly, "The prayers of the congregation reached the very throne of God in smoke—like the incense in the book of Revelation—and killed the evil spirit that tried to destroy you. Hallelujah! Thank you, God. Thank you!"

I did not know at the time that the church had been praying constantly for me. "That's right," Sister Choi said. "For the past three days they have been fasting by day and praying with tears by night."

I knew they couldn't hear me where they were, nevertheless, I said, "Thank you. Thank all of you. I was able to overcome this fiery trial only because of your prayers. Thanks to the congregation. Thank you, Reverend Hurston. I'm alive, I'm living."

Early the next morning, my coughing stopped. I still had occasional bouts of pain that left me so breathless I had to bite down on my lips until the pain stopped. In those moments, Lay Minister Choi was right next to me, calling out to the Lord for me, and sharing my very pains. I sweated so profusely it sometimes felt as if I was submerged in a pool of cold sweat. "I thank God for this trial," I said. "Now when I get back on my feet again, I shall know how to spread the Gospel. I will know the sick intimately and feel their pains. I will see their aching hearts."

"That's right," Sister Choi said, "God is going to help us."

I thanked God for the ordeal and accepted graciously what God had allowed.

Suffering is God's Sovereignty

While I was in the hospital, there was an annual meeting of the Assemblies of God in Bulkwang-dong. Unfortunately, the assembly was also going through some fiery trials and hardships. Lay Minister Choi relayed the news to me after I got out of the hospital. The assembly was on the verge of splitting up due to irreconcilable differences.

A quarrel had broken out over what to do with a plot of land near Seodae Gate. The land was purchased with a plan of building a missionary headquarters that would serve various operations in Taiwan, Tokyo, and Seoul. This dispute caused factions to form, bringing on a stalemate that lasted for six months. As a result, when Reverend Catchem, the Head of the Oriental Missions of the U.S. Assemblies of God, began the annual meeting, the atmosphere was somber and tense, and it seemed as if the assembly was on the verge of splitting. Ultimately, this dire situation led Missionary John Hurston to make a bold stance before God and the assembly.

"Korean pastors and lay ministers," he said, "you have done nothing wrong. It is our fault. We, the missionaries, will go before God and repent of our wrong doings." Missionary Hurston went down on his knees on the concrete floor where they were assembled, and cried out to God. Tears flowed in repentance. Reverends Statz and Catchem got on their knees, too. A few moments later, their spouses joined them as well in prayer and repentance. I later found out that Reverend Catchem and his wife had been praying over this issue for the past six months. That evening, the entire group of missionaries began fasting and observed an all-night prayer service, joined by friends and other members of the assembly. Their tears and this humble act of getting on their knees to repent was genuine, and it broke through the stalemate that had kept the assembly from carrying out God's plan. They earnestly sought God's forgiveness. Once the repenting missionaries took control of the meeting, everything concluded smoothly without any further mishap. Lay Minister Choi said she was so grateful that I was in the hospital while this was happening. She wholeheartedly believed that it was God's sovereign plan to hide me in a secret place where no harm would get to me.

I was so grateful when Lay Minister Choi told me everything that had happened at the meeting. I couldn't help wondering,

Dr. Cho preaching in the tent.

What if I had been at the meeting? Knowing myself, I would have stood up against the opposing group. In such circumstances, I would have felt disappointed in myself for whatever actions I may have taken and been left in emotional pain. God had led me to His place of refuge, a way out of a painful experience that I couldn't face. I prayed in gratitude for His merciful act. "I will leave the issues of the assembly in God's hands," I said to myself." May His will be done."

God knows exactly where the future leads and where I need to be at different junctures of my life. That is because He is a kind-hearted God. From a different standpoint, I appreciated the missionaries' actions, intentions, and the steadfast willpower to come to a foreign land to win over souls for God. I was overwhelmed with respect for the missionaries and their precious sacrifice as they plunged into a culture completely foreign to them in lifestyle and language, all in the name of spreading the Lord's gospel. The efforts and sacrifices of the Assemblies of God to ignite a spark for the Holy Spirit and start a movement in this country, served as water for the seed of the Gospel to grow and bear fruit for our nation and people.

Looking Toward the Seodaemun

The news of the many miracles in the tent church of Daejo-dong spread quickly. As a result, more and more people who wanted to meet the Lord came by the tent church each day. People with sicknesses came from every region to be healed. The only thing that I could do for these people who came believing that they would be cured was to pray for them. "Father God, take pity on your children, who have gathered here. Please, heal these people with the blood of Jesus and bless and change their lives."

Within four years, the church that started on the hilltop of Daejo-dong with just five people in a small room of Lay Minister Choi's home became a church with 400 members. It was a grace given to us by God for not losing hope and giving up on His idea. In spite of our ragged and ripped tent, the church was overflowing with members who wanted to hear the gospel. Also, we were able to acquire land to build a new church. At about this time, when the church was growing, God gave me another dream of developing the church. The location of that dream was the "Seodaemun" (meaning Great West Gate).

Dr. Cho working in his office.

Part 3

The Ministry in Seodaemun Church and the Encounter with the Holy Spirit

Claiming the Land in Seodaemun

On August 25, 1961, I was discharged from military service due to a severe rupture. It had been seven months since I enlisted. I returned to the church with my military style shaven head, and the congregation greeted me with smiles, and complimented me on my youthful look. I still had bandages around my abdomen from the surgeries I had undergone, and even the slightest fidgeting or tightening of the lower area of my stomach caused unbearable pain. However, the smiling faces, especially that of Lay Minister Choi's, who had stood by my side unwaveringly during my most difficult times, lessened the pain significantly.

For the first time in several months, all of us gathered at the tent church and held a service to acknowledge God for His love and grace. The tent church quickly turned into a village festival. The sound of people chatting echoed throughout the church, with laughter blossoming here and there; for the first time we felt light and peaceful, momentarily setting aside the heavy yoke and burdens we had to endure. The atmosphere was peaceful and happy, truly jolly as we served one another.

On September 1, shortly after my return, the Evangelist/Pastor Samuel J. Todd was invited to lead a tent revival in an area near Seodaemun, an area that was large enough for a circus company to hold a grand circus. As usual, I was designated as the interpreter. Despite the scorching weather, many people from all over the country flocked to the revival, surpassing our expectations. Some two hundred people with diseases and illnesses came as well.

At each revival meeting, many sick people received miraculous healings. Evangelist Todd, Lay Minister Choi, and I prayed for them by the laying on of hands. It was difficult at times to stoop down because of my surgery, and as the sharp pains surged through me, I would clasp my stomach, softly crying out to the Lord under my breath. Despite the pain, I interpreted what the evangelist said with all my conviction, strength, and passion. Even after the revival ended for the day, I had to continue leading the service at Daejo-dong tent church and help out wherever the need was great. These activities once again took a toll on my body.

This month-long great revival shook up the city, and many lost souls were led to Christ, and many sick people were healed. It was truly a God-anointed event. As for Lay Minister Choi and me, a desire to acquire the land where the revival was held, and there build our new church, flared up continually in our hearts. We might have been hallucinating, but both of us felt as if the land was calling out to us. Like Moses leading the Israelites to the Promised Land, neither of us had any doubt where our promised land was.

Seodaemun Church

At last, our church acquired some land to build a new sanctuary; and with the number of church members fairly consistent, I thought the time was ripe for them to receive a new pastor. The congregation, however, which was primarily made up of residents of Daejo-dong, reacted negatively to this idea, and were unyielding to the plan to relocate the church out of town. At first they tried to persuade us not to relocate, and some even begged not to do it, but once they saw how determined we were, they began to cook up various schemes to prevent the move from happening. Those who were opposed to the idea went around saying, "They are leaving behind the poor and the sick, and are moving inside the gate to where the rich folks are. They no longer need ignorant fools like us so they are seeking educated people for the ministry." But since we firmly believed that it was a calling from God to relocate and to start anew, we had no choice but to put up with the criticisms that came our way.

Five Sweet Potatoes for Supper

On October 15, 1961, we observed an inauguration service in Seodae Gate, the very spot where the great revival was held. The tent was already set up, which provided more than enough space for the two families in attendance. Construction had already begun on the other side of the area for the Seodae Gate Revival Center, which was expected to be completed the following year.

People slowly began flocking to the new tent church in Seodaemun. Gradually, many of the members from Daejo-dong started to come as well. The number multiplied week after week and the miraculous healings continued. Our lifestyle, however, hadn't changed much from when we lived in Daejo-dong. With some money we were able to pull together, we found a tiny place on a hilltop. It was a two-room cubbyhole, so I took one of the rooms and Sister Choi's family took the other. Our worries about the daily meals didn't go away, however, and no one was able to offer us any help, not even the missions group at the church in charge of outreach to the needy in this area. On certain nights, we only had sweet potatoes for supper. We would split these sweet potatoes among the five of us, and drink lots of water to fill our stomachs and keep us from feeling hungry. On such nights, no one said much and just tried to go to sleep. Lay Minister Choi, our anchor, prayed late into the night in her room and then left for church early in the morning when the curfew siren blew. She went there to pray in tongues and to complain to God of our hunger. You can only survive on sweet potatoes for so long, and it was becoming increasingly difficult to stave off the continual hunger that gripped us.

One morning I became overwhelmed with what I like to describe as an explosive faith in my heart. I felt it was the Holy Spirit wanting to use me as a mouthpiece to proclaim His message I stood in front of a mirror, and with my both fists clenched, and staring fiercely at myself, I began to shout:

"Yonggi Cho, you are not poor!

"Yonggi Cho, you are wealthy!

"Our church shall reach one thousand members by next year!

"Yonggi Cho, you suffered from tuberculosis in the past, but look at you now; you are healthy!

"Yonggi Cho, you have the faith to move even a mountain. Whosoever believes can achieve anything."

I suddenly sensed that I wasn't alone, so I opened the door to find Lay Minister Choi standing there. I couldn't look her in the eye because I felt pitiful and awkward, and embarrassed because I was shouting so loudly.

A Pitfall for the Self-Conceited

The change of environment when we moved the church to the new location in Seodae Gate instilled in me a new dream to build the largest church in South Korea. The largest congregation at the time housed around 6,000 members, so this challenge really sparked a fire in me. Reflecting on our church's growth from five to six hundred in three years, I knew I could expand this mid-size church into something bigger. The thought of members multiplying like a spreading wildfire captured my mind and I became somewhat pompous, seeing myself as being the center of it all and having made it happen in just three years. I was filled with self-admiration and completely forgot about God's grace. All I thought about was how capable I was, and I said to myself, "If I can gather six hundred people in three years, what can stop me from turning this church into the biggest congregation in Seoul?"

Out of curiosity, I paid a visit to the largest church with the 6,000 member congregation. I wanted to see the building for myself and even took a measuring instrument to get an accurate number. I measured the width and length of the building and walked into the main sanctuary to count the pews. It boasted a maximum occupancy of 2,000 people. I sat down and calculated my ambitious plan. I thought to myself, "I can build up my church bigger than this one, and God will be on my side to make that happen."

Early on in the ministry, God had taught me the importance of setting goals, dreaming and waiting in faith for Him to bring growth. He had taught me how to pray according to my own needs, and to envision the number of people in our congregation. In my prayers, the Holy Spirit confirmed my belief by guiding me to certain passages in the Bible, and assured me that whatever the number of people I prayed for, He would grant it to me.

In the first year, I had prayed for one hundred fifty members, and it was granted. In the following year, I asked for the number to multiply and surely enough, it did. In the third year, I asked once again for the congregation to multiply twofold and again, God listened to my prayers and the church grew to six hundred members. God listened to each of my prayer requests for more church members and granted them.

As I made plans for the next stage of growth, I decided to pray and plead with God to grow the current six hundred member congregation fivefold within three years. That meant the number of members would grow to 3,000 by 1964, so I believed it in faith, and numerically it seemed feasible.

Each time I prayed, God assured me that He had heard my prayers and I felt certain that He would grant me a church bigger than our current six hundred member church. My mind was occupied solely with expanding the church and not on what God had in store for me in order to accomplish that goal. But I had no doubt that God approved of what I was doing with the ministry. As a result, He had blessed our church with miracles

A service at Seodaemun Church.

and healings, and sent many to the church. So I began to think that God had designated me, Yonggi Cho, as a special being. God was proceeding with His plan through me. I knew that nothing could be done at the church without me. Such a thought was a fatal mistake.

The moment we had been waiting for finally arrived: the completion of the Revival Center, which could seat 1,500 people. We held the Inauguration Service on February 18, 1962. I was ordained on April 26, and on May 13 we changed the name of the church to "Central Full Gospel Church" and welcomed a brand new start. This new beginning was unmistakably wonderful. I was the Pastor, the Administrator, and in charge of the Sunday School Program. I even designated myself as the gatekeeper. I was the very cylinder that ran the maintenance and operation of the church—and relegating such duties to others was not part of what I planned.

I was born during the rule of Japanese Imperialism, and having experienced a war during my childhood, I grew up believing that I would never escape poverty and accepted this as fate. On top of that, I had tuberculosis and had come very close to dying. I wanted to overcome it all and make a name for myself to prove that my hard background was not a deterrent to my success. I even pondered an ambitious plan to become a doctor and make an unrealistically huge amount of money. I had really wanted to become an internal medicine doctor before I met Jesus Christ.

So deep down inside, even when I first stepped foot into the ministry, my ambition for fame and my passion to succeed continued to linger inside of me. Once I became a pastor, this desire came bubbling to the surface, and I harbored a hidden agenda to make a name for myself as a successful and respected preacher. I wanted to love God with all my heart and serve Him, but deep down in a secret chamber of my heart was the word "success." I was very self-centered and wanted God to do things my way. God had no choice but to demolish all that was about me. If not, the ministry would have become mine, not God's.

God had to shatter me in order to show me that I needed to serve Him with the attitude and heart of a servant and good steward over all He had given me. I was not to be confused as to who the flock of saints truly belonged to—they were His and only His.

Overworking Myself

The old year passed and the new one came and I ran relentlessly toward my goals. The year 1964 was the most formidable time for our church. The number of church members grew like yeast, fifteen or more were now coming in every week. So we had to hold four services on Sunday to accommodate all the people. If we continued at our rate of increase, by 1965 we would have approximately 7500 members. But thinking about the plan I had in mind for the church, we were still lagging behind the estimated 3000 members I had prayed to have by 1964. The total number of the congregation reached an impressive 2400 but I wasn't satisfied.

By then I was already in great distress, because I was running for the goal without looking back, and I thought God would be pleased that I was accomplishing great things for Him. I started working from early morning until late at night. I knew I was running on empty and suffering greatly from physical fatigue, but in order to sustain the momentum and vitality of the church, I had no choice but to drive myself relentlessly. I preached and counseled. I made home visits and hospital visits. I was knocking on many doors, and constantly on the run, but that was what I needed to do and I had come to accept it.

Then one particular Sunday I was confronted with a crisis. I was scheduled to conduct baptism for three hundred new believers. Missionary Hurston, who had been helping me with the ministry from the start, was standing next to me, ready to assist. However, as the nucleus of all church functions and activities, I firmly believed that I alone had to do everything. He was well aware that I was already burnt out. But that day, I told him that I would personally baptize everyone. As a special vessel of God, I believed I was the only channel for God's blessing to flow through to His people. Just as I stepped into the water to baptize the first person standing in line, Missionary Hurston came to check in on me. "Reverend Cho, I think I should take over from here." he said.

"No, that's all right. I can handle this." I replied.

But I had no strength to carry out the baptism for all those people. First I had to support the person into the water while shouting, "I baptize you in the name of the Father, the Son, and the Holy Spirit." Then I had to lift them up out of the water. I was able to carry out the first few submersions fairly well, but then some big ladies came and lifting them up out of the water took a great deal of effort. My arms felt weak. Missionary Hurston watched me with a worried look for I was pale and looking ill. I gave him a sturdy nod, signaling that I was okay and reassured him by saying, "I'm okay." But in my heart, I was desperately asking God for strength.

I baptized all three hundred believers, but when I came to the last person, I felt dizzy raising him up. I was dead tired, and yet my day wasn't done. That afternoon, I was scheduled to meet an American preacher and serve as his interpreter at the service that evening. Missionary Hurston was kindhearted and meek, a man filled with the Holy Spirit, and he expressed concern about the condition of my health. "Reverend Cho, why don't you just rest this afternoon?" he said. "I will go and meet with the preacher."

"But he is scheduled to meet with me," I replied, and shook my head and said, "No, I will meet him." I told him that as a pastor, I wanted to do everything that I was required to do. So, skipping my lunch, due to time constraints, I left for the airport to pick up the American preacher and take him to his hotel. I felt my legs quivering as I stood there next to him.

Pride of a Pastor

Many church members worried about my health but Lay Minister Choi and Missionary Hurston worried even more. The deacons decided to look for another interpreter so that I could get some rest that evening. When I heard what they planned to do, I thought to myself, "Who else can interpret for this preacher except me? I am overflowing with God's power and I am the only competent interpreter." In an effort to stop them from further pursuing the search, I yelled out to them, "No, I can do it."

It was the time for the evening service. The invited preacher began proclaiming the message. Right then, I realized he was a typical Pentecostal preacher who preaches with great energy and burning passion. He preached in a loud voice, moving around the pulpit. So I followed in his footsteps, interpreting loudly. But keeping up with him became extremely difficult as time went on, because he was a man who was powerfully anointed, and at that time I wasn't. When he heard me speak louder than him, he paused to give me a side glance and raised his voice even louder. From that point on, both of us spoke loudly, moving and jumping around the pulpit.

The atmosphere was filled with excitement, with two languages alternating simultaneously. We had been speaking for about half an hour when suddenly I felt my heart constrict and my body begin to convulse—it quickly became difficult for me to breathe and my knees began to shake. I was utterly exhausted and I knew something wasn't right. As I started to fall I heard loud screams from the pews. I was still able to hear the preacher as I fell, but my vision was fading—and then there was just darkness.

As I lay there, in the darkness that now engulfed me, I remember pleading with God, or should I say, interrogating Him. "Lord, why did you punish me before the crowd?" I asked accusingly. "You could have done this in the privacy of my office or somewhere else, where no one would see me fall on the floor." Then for a brief moment the darkness left me, and I opened my eyes and saw John Hurston and said to him, "John, I'm dying."

I heard him cry, "Pastor Cho, wake up, wake up!"

My heart was pumping rapidly as I tried desperately to breathe. It felt as if my entire body, all my veins and tissues were begging for oxygen. I lost consciousness. When I came back to

Billy Graham preaching in the Yoido Full Gospel Church with Dr. Cho as an interpreter.

consciousness, I tried to get up to the pulpit again. I pressed down with my legs and gathered my strength to lift myself up, but then I realized the service was over, and paramedics had already arrived to take me to a hospital.

I was ashamed to be a pastor. I prayed for the sick and they were healed by God's grace, but I just couldn't deal with this on a personal level. I insisted that I would heal myself and thought it was the right thing to do. I was certain God would heal me miraculously and send me home from the hospital. "Please release me from the hospital," I said. "I trust in God's words, 'by His stripes we were healed.'"

I declined any injections and medicine. Even the doctors were unable to change my mind. The doctor released me from the hospital because I refused any treatment, and so the deacons took me home. But there was no sign of God healing me. I recited the passages in the Bible where it promises healing, I pleaded with God to heal me, then I demanded that He heal me. Lying there on my bed in the apartment, I searched for all the passages and references about healing in the Bible, even the indirect references, and demanded God's intervention. I cited all the Bible verses I knew as well as the ones I had found. "God, these are your promises," I said. "You cannot turn away from your promises—I should be healed in the name of your Son, Jesus."

But there were no signs of healing. I struggled to breathe. There were a number of deacons in the church who were doctors, but I turned down their care as well. "I shall stand firmly on your word, and on your promises," I declared to God.

That was what I said. It was the arrogance of a pastor who had only reason, not faith. It was then that I realized a valuable lesson about the difference of a life of faith based on reason and a life of faith based on faith. As I cited and quoted those passages in reference to healing, I approached it in its *logos* form. The word of God in *logos* form is applicable to all humanity. But whenever I make my demands known to God, I take possession of His word and personalize them. If done right, the Holy Spirit grants a special confirmation to the heart. I finally learned that I must seize His word that can pierce even the division of soul and spirit and make it my own. That is how one gains faith even to move a mountain.

For a while, I was in denial of certain symptoms I was experiencing. The thought that I could be bedridden never crossed my mind. I made an earnest effort not to pay attention to the spirit of death hovering in the room. I had no intention of giving up.

Gearing Up for Another Phase in the School of Pastoral Ministry

After some rest, I greatly desired to stand behind the pulpit the following Sunday, and with the help of some deacons, I stood before the congregation, quivering and feeling weak all over. In a soft, low voice I began preaching, but not for long. I stuttered confusedly and for about eight minutes proclaimed the message, and then fainted. When I became conscious, I began to quote the passages. *"And by His stripes we were healed; He knew our weaknesses, so He bore the burden himself."* But in my heart, there was no confirmation from the Holy Spirit that I would be cured. I stood before the congregation for the second service. I prayed to God for strength, but that time I only lasted five minutes.

I was taken home, and I thought the time had come for me to move on—either to another work or to Heaven. At that moment, I was enlightened with another discovery: God cannot work if I recklessly spread all of my problems before Him. Meditating on this thought, it dawned on me that up until that moment I had not sought God's will for my circumstances. In other words, I didn't consider the fact that perhaps healing me wasn't really part of God's plan. So I went to God and asked Him, "God, you gave us all of your promises. I made my requests, but you did not respond. Are you really not going to heal me?"

I was literally shocked when moments later, I heard an unusual response from God. *"Son, I will heal you, but it is going to take ten years."*

I looked around the room. The voice was unusually clear and near, so I knew I wasn't hallucinating. I was overcome with an indescribable peace in my heart. I really desired to argue with God but, at the same time I somehow knew that wasn't an option.

During the ten year period, I experienced many moments of tremendous suffering—even to the point of death. God had a plan to break down my will and my stubborn heart, but ten years seemed too long to me. If that was His plan, to bring me down from my high self-regard as the "Great Yonggi Cho," I greatly wished He would do it in a moment's notice.

It is too difficult for me to explain in detail all the painful experiences I endured in that ten year period. Every morning when I woke up, I had to closely monitor my heart to make sure it wasn't beating too hard. I had to fight off this sense that some gruesome force of death was creeping up from my toes. In order to console myself, I thought about God's promise to heal me.

My ambitions to build the biggest church in South Korea quickly vanished, I even began to doubt that I could possibly reach that goal—or that there was any way I could ever reach it. At times, I even doubted whether or not I could continue to minister to the congregation of 2400 people. However, because of God's promise, I had to ward off any thought of throwing in the towel. During this period of time, Reverend Hurston preached from the pulpit on my behalf, and because I wished to be sitting behind the pulpit, I had to rely on the help of the deacons to climb onto the rostrum.

Due to such dire and desperate circumstances, I began to realize that God might have something greater in store for me. As I endured the pains, I had a feeling that I was being trained for something greater—a magnificently grand plan. I slowly realized that God was in control of my life. I was placed in His hands, and He would command and control me. I had to accept this and brace myself for it. Thankfully, that was around the time when God's plan for me and the Central Full Gospel Church were about to unfold. I had no idea that we were being prepared to be in His plan. God had me enrolled in the "School of the Wilderness" all along, and I was about to graduate from it. At the same time, God enrolled me into another school: the "School of Pastoral Ministry."

The First Course: The Holy Spirit and Healing

About a month after I collapsed, God began correcting my wrong ways of carrying out the ministry. Lying there helpless, I made a solemn oath not to give up on the ministry no matter what the cost. Reverend Hurston and Lay Minister Choi took it upon themselves to carry out the ministry work; it was quite a burden to meet the needs of the 2400 member congregation.

At that time South Korea was still a poor country, and the responsibility of the laity to finance the ministry from their own scarce earnings was taking its toll. I knew I had to keep finding ways to motivate God's people to become more active around the church and to participate in various programs and ministries, but I didn't know where to begin.

The days when I lay in bed recuperating, there wasn't much I could do on my own. Physically, I was burnt out and exhausted, and my heart, once thriving with zeal and passion, was in the doldrums. I felt like discarded trash lying there on the bed. I was in no condition to go on any outings without assistance since I was still extremely weak and would pass out.

My daily routine consisted of sleeping and praying; however, I wasn't praying just any ordinary prayer. I was praying to keep from death's door as death knocked on the door of my conscience. I prayed desperately for God to help me overcome this adversity.

My bedridden state also opened up other doors as I pondered what more I could do to help the ministry. I began to pay more attention to the Bible and dove into an in-depth study of the

Bible. Looking back now, I can see that God was preparing me so that I could be used for His greater glory.

God used that time of intensive Bible study to start me on the first course of the School of Pastoral Ministry. The name of the course was "The Holy Spirit and Healing." From the pulpit and elsewhere, I spoke adamantly and passionately about the power of healing, especially after seeing with my own eyes the miraculous healings that God brings forth. But summoning that same power for my own circumstances seemed difficult. It was around this time that I also realized that I didn't have much biblical knowledge on this topic, though I had many scriptural references. It became crystal clear to me then just how important it was to have a close and personal relationship with the Holy Spirit so He can teach you the truths of the Word of God.

Throwing myself into learning, and researching the topic of healing subsequently led me to publish books. My first book

Dr. Cho's books have been translated into many languages.

was entitled, *Jesus Christ, the Healer* and the second book, *The Holy Spirit*. Through my studies, I began to see my faith grow and my knowledge increase. I was becoming quite an expert on passages relating to the Holy Spirit.

We often hear that we need to have fellowship with God the Father and Jesus the Son, but it was only after I studied the Bible extensively that I discovered we need to have *"communion with the Holy Spirit"* (2 Corinthians 13:14). To my surprise, I learned that communion is achieved on a deeper level than through fellowship. One dictionary defined *communion* as an *"intimate relationship accompanied by an in-depth understanding"* and in another source, *"the act of sharing ones' ideas and feelings with another."* God spoke to me about the importance of having an intimate communion with the Holy Spirit; that is, to share my deep thoughts and feelings with Him.

The Lord said this to me: *"Think about marriage. When a man marries a woman, he takes her into his home and does not leave her. He does not treat the woman as a material possession, he shares his life intimately with her. This is the type of relationship you need to have with the Holy Spirit."*

From 1964 to 1965, I had to spend most of my time in bed due to my illness, but it was also during this time that my communion with the Holy Spirit deepened and took on more meaningful characteristics. I wrote two books and both of them became best sellers in Korea and Japan. I realized, however, that that was just a taste of what was to come, and that realization gave me great strength to carry on my pastoral ministry work. The most important lesson God taught me during this time was that I needed to farm out more of my responsibilities to other church workers, entrusting them with ministerial duties and responsibilities.

Church Within the Family

Lying in my bed, I kept thinking about how I could continue to minister to my congregation in a more dynamic fashion. *"What if the church grows in size?"* I thought. *"What do I do then?"* I began questioning the Holy Spirit, engaging Him in an intimate communion. "Lord, what do I need to do? How can I achieve this?"

"Let my people depart first," He said, *"then let them grow."*

I was shocked to hear those words. I didn't know how to respond. "What does this mean?" I wondered.

The Holy Spirit continued to speak, *"Let my people leave the 'Palace of Yonggi Cho.' Once they do, support them and help them grow."*

"Yes, Lord," I said. "But what do you mean by letting them grow?"

"Help and guide them so that they may stand on their own two feet. Help them start their own ministries." He replied.

His voice compelled me to search the Scriptures. I looked up the epistles written by the Apostle Paul. Ephesians 4:11 states, "And He himself gave some to be apostles, some prophets, some evangelists, and some pastors and teachers" and in verse 12, "for the equipping of the saints [apostles, prophets, gospel sharers, pastors, and teachers] for the work of ministry, for the edifying of the body [the laity] of Christ" (see also Acts 2:46-47, NKJV)

This is why the laity can work in and out of the church in their ministries—I was encouraged by reading this. The meetings that took place during the age of the apostolic Church occurred in two places:

1. The disciples met regularly and consistently in the temples, and

2. In their homes to break bread and have fellowship.

During the time of the apostolic Church, some 100,000 Christians of the 200,000 people living in Jerusalem belonged to the Church. There were only twelve apostles at the time, so who was actually looking after the multitude? Could the twelve possibly visit their homes individually to minister to them? They couldn't have. So I came to the conclusion that there had to be some small, inner, groups who were working alongside the apostles to help manage the load. Like the seven deacons who appear in Acts 6, they must have shared the work of visiting homes with the apostles. In other words, they themselves created small groups or *cell groups* to have their fellowship.

Up until that time, I firmly believed that the congregation should only be gathering at the church sanctuary. I had never considered the possibility of turning family households into a church. But the Scriptures clearly and poignantly demonstrate a case for households to be a meeting place for God's people. I thought about our church and the ministries we had—we had no ministry in place to carry out home visits, so I insisted that they come to church on Sundays and Wednesdays. Little did I know that this was a weak point for us in carrying out a more effective ministry.

The Holy Spirit led me to meditate on Acts 6. In that passage the apostles elected deacons, like Stephen and others filled with the Holy Spirit, to carry out the ministry and to be fishers of men for God. The apostles limited their ministry work by devoting themselves only to prayer and spreading the gospel. But when Stephen, one of the seven deacons, was martyred and stoned to death, the Church scattered. Then in Acts 8, in reference to Philip's movement to spread the gospel, we see that deacons also started taking on the role of preaching the gospel.

The apostles not only commissioned certain leaders to take on the authority of ministering to other Christians, but to preach the gospel as well.

After carefully examining the Book of Acts, I realized that some 3,000 people entered the Church on the day of Pentecost and 5,000 more the following day. I also knew that there were only twelve apostles and seven deacons. The apostles selected leaders not only to lead and attend household meetings, but also to have time for fellowship, so many more Christians were able to receive care from the Church. Building on the momentum from the reorganization, and assigning of some of the ministerial responsibilities to the laity, the Church was better able to look after the needs of Christians. "That's it!" I exclaimed, as a light came on inside my head.

Reading the Scriptures, I discovered that another kind of "church" was formed from those household meetings. In other words, I realized what makes up a "cell group." We see manifestations of a cell group church at the homes of Lydia (Acts 16:40), Priscilla and Aquila (Romans 16:3-5), and Philemon (Philemon 1:2). Most assuredly, the Scriptures provide ample evidence to support household meetings as being biblical.

Jethro's Advice, Entrusting Others with Authority

In Exodus 18, I saw that Moses alone addressed the grievances of the Israelites and offered wise counsel. From morning till night, he alone listened to their quarrels and made decisions on matters. Jethro, his father-in-law, saw that the lengthy process was taking a toll on Moses, so he taught Moses how to" not get burnt out" from fulfilling his duties, while at the same time meeting everyone's needs.

"Moreover, you shall select from all the people able men, such as fear God, men of truth, hating covetousness; and place such over them to be rulers of thousands, rulers of hundreds, rulers of fifties, and rulers of tens. And let them judge the people at all times. Then it will be that every great matter they shall bring to you, but every small matter, they themselves shall judge. So it will be easier for you, for they will bear the burden with you" (Exodus 18:21-22, NKJV).

From the Scriptures, I started to understand the process of electing leaders and entrusting them with God-ordained authority and power. Slowly, my mind began to race with a plan, I thought, "What if I, too, send out deacons who will open their homes and make them accessible to the lost? What if the deacons went around teaching, praying for the sick for healing, serving and supporting, and helping each other within these groups? The church would flourish within these homes!" If everything went the way I envisioned it, the laity would invite their friends and acquaintances to those meetings and use the occasion to witness to them. On Sundays the laity would invite the newcomers to the church to take part in the service. With more members around the church, I can offer up more opportunities for them to serve, thereby assigning responsibilities, which then would release me from much of the time-consuming work of making home visits and counseling.

I made a firm vow: I will devote my time to educate, lead, and preach to the laity and leave myself open to God, so that He can use me elsewhere to carry out His will. For three weeks I devised an all-out plan to revitalize the church. I also knew that I would need to receive consent from the Deacon Board before this plan could be carried out. This point was all the more crucial as I was very aware of how important it was to achieve a consensus, especially since I had heard rumors that the deacons were beginning to question my leadership.

My ailing health continued to be a problem. I was able to get out of bed on my own but it was another matter altogether to be able to stand on my own. When I went to see the doctor, he strongly and compellingly advised me to consider stepping down from the ministry. "Pastor, you have a very weak heart and your entire system is quite weak. You are suffering from nervous tension and exhaustion. The only helpful advice I can give you is to quit your ministry,"

"Isn't there any medicine that I can take?" I asked.

"No," he replied. "I'm afraid not. Actually, there isn't anything wrong with you physically. But you worked too hard for too long. Simply put, you are burnt out from stress. The weakness and the tremors you experience in your heart are from overworking yourself all those years. It's purely psychological, Pastor. If there is any medicine, it would be that you need to find work that is less strenuous, both emotionally and physically."

It felt like he had given me a death sentence—how could I give up my pastoral ministry, my lifetime calling? I wasn't ready to give up without a fight. I knew God wasn't through with me yet, and that He had a plan to build up a great church. It would take ten years before God healed me completely. But in the meantime, I had to bank on the promise that He made. Once again I put my absolute confidence in God the healer rather than in the physician.

Motivation Remodeling

Then came the great day when God revealed His great plan to renovate the church and the laity so that the burden of carrying the ministry was no longer solely on my shoulders. This revelation brought great joy and anticipation to the heart of this twenty-eight-year-old man, whose body was already worn out, and who was given no hope by earthly physicians.

When my heart recovered somewhat, I began to prepare myself for the day when I would return to the church and reveal this new plan to the congregation. However, I knew that I couldn't just lay this out to the 2400 plus members and have them execute it like some military command. Also, the Deacon Board, from whom I needed to gain approval to carry out this plan, had gone through quite some change while I was out and was keeping me on my toes. "Lord," I said, "this is your plan. How could they not accept a plan coming from you?"

A month later, I returned to the church and called a meeting with the Deacon Board and began to share with them: "As you all know, I'm quite ill. I am in no position to carry out every facet of the pastoral ministry, such as doing home visits and counseling. Also, I cannot lay my hands on sick people, even on healthy ones, so that they may be filled with the Holy Spirit."

With this introduction, I shared my thoughts with the board and explained all the scriptural passages that God had revealed to me. I told them that their role was pivotal in executing this new kind of ministry, and shared with them the same plan God had shown me. I tried to explain to the deacons what a cell group was and how it worked. I even gave them the entire scriptural basis for initiating a cell group meeting. Then I waited for the many responses I expected to get.

One said, "That seems to be right, Pastor, you have many supports from the Bible."

Another said, "I can see that this indeed came from our Lord."

And there was the expected response, "We aren't really trained to do what you are able to do. That is why we look up to you as our pastor and why we compensate you."

Another deacon spoke up. "I'm an extremely busy person. When I return home from work, I'm very tired. I need my private life at home. I just don't have the time or the energy to lead, a … what is it, yeah … a cell group."

Everyone agreed that forming a cell group seemed like a good idea, but they weren't able to foresee how this would impact and benefit the church in the long run. I was frustrated at being unable to explain this new idea effectively. No one rejected the idea outright, but it was clear to me that this plan wouldn't come to fruition. Even though the deacons didn't voice their gut reaction, I picked up on what they were thinking as I listened and paid attention to their nonverbal reactions. In their minds, I was being compensated essentially for this function so the idea of their having to do my job, so to speak, and without pay, seemed unacceptable. I had to be careful not to have them think that I was using my illness as an excuse to pass off my job.

In my eyes, it also didn't seem like the deacons had much sympathy toward my physical condition. After the meeting, I heard from an inside source that the board considered replacing me with another pastor if I pursued the agenda any further. If they so chose, they could have justified it by a lack of confidence in my execution of my pastoral duties. I couldn't dismiss this idea entirely from the numerous options they had at their disposal. On top of all this, I also knew that I had to take into consideration my physical condition, since I was still very weak.

Women in Leadership Conflict

I went to see the only person who would listen to my concerns and problems. I met with Lay Minister Choi and told her everything. We prayed together, read the Word, and shared many ideas and alternative plans to initiate cell group meetings. Also we privately discussed the idea of tapping into the women members of the church and utilizing them to be leaders of cell groups. As I was deeply meditating and praying about the plan, Lay Minister Choi spoke up softly. "I believe that this is indeed God's plan, and I'm certain that He revealed it to you for this very reason. I think I ought to start searching for some faithful female deacons around the church and share this plan with them."

I nodded in agreement. But a part of me knew that we were treading on dangerous ground; the possibility of success seemed quite slim. Who would accept such a proposal, let alone understand it? Also, I had cultural issues to consider in following this path. In Korea, the culture dictates that women are required to be obedient and submissive. For thousands of years, Korean men demanded absolute submission from Korean women. No woman had ever taken on a leading role in Korean churches, let alone in a societal role.

I must admit that I, too, had a difficult time trying to comprehend this bold plan—a historically unprecedented move. How could women lead fellowship meetings in their households? Is it even possible? The men would seriously object to it. Also, don't the Scriptures say women need to be silent in the church? Wasn't that what the Apostle Paul wrote to Timothy in 2 Timothy 2:11?

As an Asian, I had a keen sense of what Paul was really trying to teach his protégé Timothy. When Paul wrote the epistle to Timothy, he must have written it with an Oriental mindset. Reading the passage in reference to women being silent in the church, I saw the correlation to Korean society as a whole. At the time, many Korean churches divided up the men and women so that the men sat on the right side of the pews and women on the left. A large curtain would hang down from the ceiling right in the middle of the pews to prevent them from seeing each other. Toward the end of the service, some women who were anxious to leave would move in close to the edge of the pews, near the curtains and whisper to their husbands, "Are you there, honey? Are you ready to go? I'll meet you out by the mail box." At times, their disturbance was so frequent that the pastor would say, "Ladies, please remain silent until you are outside the church."

The apostle Paul knew the relevance of the word "lord" when he references the times Sarah addresses Abraham. In those times, a woman would address her husband as "lord." Similarly, if you asked a Korean woman about her husband's wellbeing in those days, she would surely respond, "Yes, my lord is doing well. Thank you."

As I thought more about this matter, I couldn't help but wonder whether this idea of raising up women leaders came from my own thoughts or from God. I prayed, "God, are you going to let the people rise up to oppose your plan and ruin your church? Everyone will turn their backs on me if I keep encouraging women to take up the leadership roles."

The Lord spoke back to me very clearly. *"Yes, that is your thought. But raising up the women and using them is part of my plan."*

"Lord," I said, "if you insist on using them, you must show me proof from the Scriptures as your confirmation." God and I were in a tug-o-war.

Approval of Women in Leadership
For the next few days, I diligently searched the Scriptures. I asked God to show me the verses and passages to support the use of women as leaders. Gradually, God began showing me a new picture. I realized that Paul was not the male chauvinist that he

is sometimes mistakenly portrayed as being. On the contrary, Paul had many women as his ministry partners; but the women's ministry was carried out solely under his headship.

The literal reading of Romans 16:1 calls Phoebe a deacon in the church at Cenchrea, which means that she held a leadership role at her church. But she was under the headship of the Apostle Paul. When he entrusted Phoebe with overseeing the Roman church, it is clear that she not only served but also had the responsibility to preach. Paul commissioned her to proclaim the message, which meant she was free to lead a ministry of her own.

In Romans 16:3-5, Paul mentions Priscilla and Aquila, and speaks of "the church that is in their house." Who was doing the preaching in their house? I conjured up what might have happened in those days with the oriental mindset. In the Oriental discourse, the name of the leader is always mentioned first, which means that Priscilla's name doesn't come first just because they are following polite manners of putting ladies first. If a Westerner walked into an Asian household and greeted the wife first, rather than the husband, such an act would seriously insult the family. In a Korean household, the same principle applies. If a visitor stops by the house when the man of the house isn't there, it is customary for the visitor to first inquire about the well being of her husband by asking, "How is your husband doing?" After that, the visitor can greet the wife by saying, "Hello." The husband always comes first because he is the head of the household.

In Korea, we don't use phrases like "ladies and gentlemen." Such an expression would sound very awkward. Instead, we say, "gentlemen and ladies." In Korea, men don't stand behind women or hold the doors open for them. The women wait for the men to walk through first and then follow them in. Such a practice is the custom of the Orient.

When Paul writes "Priscilla and Aquila," we need to examine the order of the names and understand the reasoning in the context of Paul's times. Priscilla was Aquila's wife but the Holy Spirit inspired Paul to mention her name before his. But why? I believe it is because she was the leader of the church that met in their household. In other words, Priscilla was the "pastor" and Aquila was her assistant. Because Paul commissioned Priscilla, and not Aquila, with leadership and authority, she was able to carry out the ministry of leading their home-based church.

Romans 16:6 says, "Greet Mary, who labored much for us." She is mentioned here as a servant of God, not some lady who works in the kitchen or changes diapers. The women Paul mentions were working by his side to proclaim the good news of the gospel. Tryphena and Tryphosa mentioned in Romans 16:12 belonged to that same group and were called "laborers in Christ," not women who took care of household chores. In that same verse, Paul mentioned Persis who "labored much in the Lord."

How do people become servants of God? They become witnesses of Christ, pray with others, proclaim the Word, and help others who are in need physically and spiritually. Such passages revealed a wealth of evidence that clearly God was using women for His purpose.

Leadership Under the Headship of the Pastor

The Scripture recognizes women leadership but only under the headship of men, especially under the authority of the apostles. For example, Paul charges every woman to cover her head when she prophesies (1 Corinthians 11:5) and if she didn't cover her head, Paul said that she "dishonors her head." The women were free to prophesy, but they also had to keep in mind that prophesying was a form of preaching. They also had to demonstrate in their messages that they were still under the headship of men.

Then the Lord spoke to me again. *"Yonggi Cho, how did you come into this world?"* He asked.

"From a woman, Lord." I replied.

"On whose lap were you brought up?" He asked.

"A woman's, Lord," I said.

"Who made the great effort to fulfill my needs, and who remained faithful to the end of my ministry?"

"They were women."

The Lord continued, *"And who came to my tomb to sprinkle oil on my body?"*

"A woman, Lord."

"Who first witnessed my resurrection?"

"A woman."

"And after I resurrected, to whom did I first appear?"

"It was Mary Magdalene, Lord, a woman."

"You've answered 'woman' to all of my questions. Then what are you afraid of? Devoted and loyal women surrounded me during my public life and ministry. Why can't my Body be surrounded by dedicated women and their support?"

What other confirmation did I need to proceed with this plan? He had clearly shown me that He approved of delegating leadership roles to women in the Church.

Birth of Twenty Groups and a Hat Episode

After that special lecture on women directly from the Lord, I called a meeting the following week with the entire women's group from our church. Some twenty women sat in the meeting room, anxiously waiting to hear what I had to say. I told them frankly about some of my own personal problems due to illness, my plans to form cell groups, and my desire to use women in the ministry, backing up my claims with biblical passages.

"My health is on the brink. Ladies, you need to help me strengthen this Body of Christ. God desires to use women for His work. Many women helped Jesus during His earthly ministry and were with Him during His hardest moments. I believe it is the will of God for you to lead cell groups."

"Amen," they replied. "What you are saying is right. It is the will of God. We will help."

The men at the previous meeting had reacted very logically and rationally. The women, on the other hand, were very passionate about the plan. They were gravely concerned about my health and unanimously agreed to follow my lead. Lay Minister Choi was relegated the responsibility of organizing the groups. Under her leadership, these dedicated women created twenty different districts within Seoul city, which matched the number of women present at the meeting. Finally, the long awaited cell groups were born.

I also made another request of them. Like Paul charging every woman to cover her head, I requested that all women leaders, including Lay Minister Choi, wear a hat as a mark of subordination and recognition of the headship of their pastor. I also wanted the church members to see that they were ministering under God's authority invested through me. Applying these biblical principles turned out to be a good idea and I met with no obstacles.

Excruciating pain in my body continued to remind me that I was still very ill. But that evening I returned home with a wonderful sense of exuberance and excitement, anticipating where this God-led initiative would actually end up. I told myself that at last all my worries and concerns were over.

Marriage to Sung Hye Kim

God gave me the greatest gift I could ever have, which is my wife. When I think about that time, I cannot help but to be in awe of His plans for me. This is because even while I was in seminary, God was already preparing my future bride. How is this possible you may ask? It is because He is God.

Mother Pastor Choi had a daughter who attended Ewha Women's University; her name was Sung Hye Kim. My first meeting with Sunghye was very refreshing. One time when I was in seminary, I got very sick with a high fever after getting a haircut and going to the public bathhouse on a cold winter day. Mother Pastor came to me to take care of me while I was sick. While she was opening the door to my room, she heard God speaking to her, *"This will be your son-in-law, so take good care of him."*

"What?" she said.

"Pray well for your son-in-law." God said.

She couldn't believe it, "It can't be; they have such a big age difference." She felt like she had been shocked by electricity. At the time, I was twenty-one and her daughter was only sixteen and in middle school.

Soon after that, I heard news that Sunghye, who lived in Jinhae was coming to visit her mother during summer vacation. I felt like she was my sister because she was the daughter of Lay Minister Choi, whom I treated like a mother. With a feeling of welcome, I went looking for them in the dorm rooms.

"Mother! I heard Sunghye is here from Jinhae." I said.

"No," she replied, "No one is here."

"That's very strange." I replied. "I definitely heard that she was here. Her shoes are here, too." I looked around the area and went into the room. A few moments later, someone came out of the closet.

"Mom! It's hot in there. Why did you push me into the closet?" Sunghye said, as she came out of the closet complaining to her mother.

I laughed when I saw her coming out of the closet. The situation was funny to me, and Sunghye also looked so adorable walking out of the closet.

This was my first meeting with Sunghye. After that first meeting, we became as close as siblings. Sunghye had a special gift for music. From the time of the tent church in Daejo-dong she has played the piano for our church. And while she was attending Ewha Women's University, she taught piano lessons to fund her tuition.

As time went on, I felt my heart open up to Sunghye and I realized that I was attracted to her. I was pleased to discover that the attraction was mutual, and that she had feelings for me. I decided that I would ask Sunghye to marry me and be my lifetime companion. One day, I called her into my office. It felt a bit strange since we were close, almost like siblings, but I gathered the courage to tell her what was in my heart. "Sunghye! You've passed. I've been closely watching you for the past few years, and you've won my approval to be my wife."

"Me? Your wife?" She seemed very surprised at my proposal.

I gave her a watch as an engagement gift. A year and a half from that day, on March 1, 1965, at the age of thirty, I married Sunghye, who was six years younger than me at that time, because of when our birthdays came in the year. We happily planned our wedding, but on our wedding day I was quite ill and wasn't able to fully enjoy this momentous occasion. I begged God for strength to get me through the day, but felt quite jittery for most of the day. Over three thousand people attended our wedding ceremony. We had invited a missionary to be the moderator and officiator. He preached for nearly an hour, entranced by his own words of encouragement for the new couple. The guests were starting to get uncomfortable, and I kept fidgeting, doing whatever I could to prevent myself from passing out. My desperate attempt to stand still was the only memory I have of that day. Quite honestly, I don't even remember what I said as my wedding vows.

During our honeymoon, my poor wife did nothing but take care of me to improve my health. As for me, my thoughts were focused on the church, especially on our newly formed cell groups. I hoped that we had cleared all the major hurdles.

Our time spent as newlyweds was quite brief since I was scheduled to speak at various revival meetings for the next six months throughout the rural areas in the country. By that time, I was one of the most widely-known pastors in South Korea.

Dr. Cho, his wife and their three sons.

During the week I was out of town preaching somewhere, and returned to Seoul only to lead our church service on Sunday, and then head right back out that very evening for another week of speaking engagements. At times, it was difficult for Sunghye to deal with my travel schedule, let alone expect a blissful newlywed phase. The only thing I brought back from my travels was a suitcase full of dirty laundry. Now I knew what people meant when they said that a pastor's wife takes up the cross of hardship and sacrifice.

My wife endured many hardships as a pastor's wife for a three-year period—for example, I received no financial compensation from the church during the time of renovation and expansion. So in order to make ends meet, my wife began giving piano lesson. I'd frequently get home to find a big placard, "Private Piano Lesson," hanging on the door as she gave private lessons.

World-Renowned Story of Our Church Growth Explosion

The cell groups grew and multiplied, which impacted the church growth. The cell groups were a role model of what a successful ministry should be. The cell group members invited their neighbors and acquaintances to the group meetings, and through them non-believers were accepting Christ into their hearts. When it became large enough, the cell group would split into two new cell groups and separate. That way it multiplied like body cells undergoing mitosis or meiosis. Every Sunday, we saw the membership grow in numbers and many continued to flock to the church. As the cell group numbers grew we had to raise up more leaders to oversee the cell groups and appoint more men and women deacons to take on this role. The church grew to the point where I couldn't estimate its size. We hadn't been keeping count on the number of members, but an official tabulation we did in 1964 showed that our church had 2,400 members; how many we had now we did not know, we only knew it was far beyond that number. We attributed the growth to the active cell groups—but none of us knew the exact number or even bothered to keep track.

The demanding schedule often took a toll on my fragile condition. There were many days when I felt like I was standing on the brink of death. I remember often praying this prayer: "Lord, just let me preach one more time and then I would be happy to die." Even in such conditions, God led me to travel throughout the world. Word of the growth of our church spread like wildfire and attracted the world's attention. Not just well known in Korea, the explosion of growth excited even the Assemblies of God denomination in the United States. Right then, I began to envision the world as a stage to start cell groups. I was appointed the Chairman of the Assemblies

Altar Call at a crusade in Yokohama, Japan.

Crowds gathering for a crusade of Dr. Cho.

of God in Korea and took part in preparing for the World's Pentecostal Conferences held in Seoul and Brazil; I also served on its advisory committee. Our church was devoted entirely to spreading the missions outreach programs throughout the world and I was busy planting cell groups in those ministries.

Brokenness in Leadership

The church continued to experience astronomical growth, but my health wasn't improving at all. I passed out in the most unexpected places. One time I fainted at the Tokyo Airport, and another time at the Assemblies of God Conference in America. Once I was in Singapore at a district office when I collapsed. On all those occasions, I felt sorry for my wife, having to go through such great distress.

I continued to pray for the sick and they received healing. Every time I witnessed God's awesome healing power, I would plead with Him to heal me. "Lord, what about me? Please don't forget to heal your servant." But God had told me that it would take ten years before I would be fully healed and, indeed, it took ten long years for me to fully recover.

I realized it was foolish for me to believe I had everything under control. How could I think such a thing? Why was I in such great pain? I had once dreamed of making a name for myself, for my own glory. I wanted to build the world's largest church. Now I knew that the only thing that mattered was completely trusting in God and relying on Him for everything—my life, health, and hope. God, in His merciful grace, showed His great affection toward me.

I realize now that God used those painful experiences to break me. I understand why the leader must be thoroughly shattered and broken. If for whatever reason the leader cannot be broken to become humble, I'm afraid he's in no position to take on the calling of being the shepherd of God's sheep. He wouldn't be able to lead God's people. Why? Because he would always live in fear and it will take control of his life.

An unbroken leader is often afraid of losing his authority or leadership, so he often thinks about filling that void with money or power. He would never trust his own congregation, and wouldn't exercise his leadership or headship over the church out of fear of losing his authority and influence. He would be worried constantly that he might make a mistake before his congregation and become a laughingstock—and even be kicked out of his church.

God uses people only to the extent that they are broken. I know that God cannot use me unless I'm completely shattered and broken. Until I get to a point where I no longer rely on my own strength but His, God cannot use me. So after ten long years of suffering, I learned how insignificant I was, and I realized just how helpless I was without God's help.

Rendering of Yoido Full Gospel Church.

Part 4

The World's Largest Church

A Swarm of Bees Flying Through a Sandstorm

I was resting in my office one Sunday morning after leading a worship service, when I heard a knock on the door. A voice outside the door said, "Pastor?" It was a deaconess from the church, a quiet woman who has been faithfully praying for my ministry. "Come on in," I said. "How was the service today?"

"I'm always blessed and moved by your preaching, Pastor," she replied. "I really like your sermons. I'm truly grateful."

"Thanks to your prayers," I said. "But what brings you here today? Is there something wrong?"

"Well," she said. "I had a dream a few days ago, and it just keeps popping up in my head. I prayed about the dream, and the more I pray about it, the clearer and clearer it gets, like a scene from a movie."

"What was it about?" I said. "Tell me about the dream."

"It was about bees," she said. Then she told about her dream in detail like Joseph had told about his dreams. "There were all these bee hives on a hill, and the bees were busily transferring honey from nearby flowers to the hives. All of sudden, all the scattered bees huddled up; I had never seen so many bees in one place in my life. The swarm of bees began flowing rapidly in one direction—toward the church. It was so strange I decided to follow them.

"I ran after the swarm of bees like I had my own pair of wings. When I got close to the church I saw the bees begin flying around it. When I reached the church, I just stood there watching them fly round and round. Then all of a sudden they left the church and flew elsewhere. So I followed them again. After some time, a river appeared. The bees flew across it, but I couldn't without wings. I wanted to follow. I yelled out to them to take me along, but my plea got drowned out by their massive humming noise. I had no choice but to stand there and watch them as long as I could."

"Is that everything?" I asked.

"Yes, that's all," she said, "But Pastor, I knew for certain that the direction they flew was toward Yoido. Their number was just massive, and it's the same scene I get every time I pray about it."

The deaconess told about the dream excitedly several times that day. And each time I heard it, her body movement, and her tone of voice convinced me that it was something that she had actually witnessed in her dream.

After she left, I began thinking about the dream and her passion in telling it. The more I thought about it, I realized the event was quite out of the ordinary. I then thought that God might be telling me something through that dream. So I prayed and earnestly sought God about the dream, like Joseph did when he had his dreams and asked God to interpret them for him. God answered my prayer for interpretation just as he did for the dream Joseph had of the cupbearer and the baker. The dream about the swarm of bees was symbolic of the future of our church. Are you ready to hear the story—and how it all got started?

The Story of the Building of the Yoido Church

Around the time the deaconess came to see me about the dream the church at Seodaemun was experiencing a huge growth in members. Some 10,000 members attended the Sunday services. No churches in Korea, at the time, had that many people coming to their services. God really enabled us to grow—it was a great revival.

Then one day God spoke to me about what was to be the Yoido church. *"Yonggi! Build a church that can house 10,000 at one time for a service! Build a church that will send out 500 missionaries to take the gospel to the world!"* I was just shocked at what I heard. The size of church He was telling me to build was unprecedented in Korea.

"How do I build a church that big?" I asked.

"You just obey me." He replied.

God instilled His word in me, "The lot is cast into the lap, but its every decision is from the LORD" (Proverbs 16:33, NKJV). It wasn't me building the church. If God willed it, He will build it. I just dream it. So I obeyed. "Amen! I will do it," I said. "I will obey your word and build that church."

Once I decided to do what God said to me, I started thinking about the ideal place to build it. After I searched for several days, the land in Yoido caught my eye. The sandy Island of Yoido, at the time, was being used as a United States Air Base. Unlike other areas, which were either too small or pricey, the land on Yoido was big and cheap. After some thought, I decided to go with Yoido. However, all the money the church had at the time was only $1,000. It was a measly amount, too small to even use as a security deposit on a rent.

Once the decision had been made, I decided to consult a construction company. I told them about my vision for a church. The owner told me to forget about it. "Pastor! To build a church that big, you would need $2,000,000. How much do you have?" he asked.

"Uh ... well, let's see ... about $1,000," I said.

The man just sat there staring at me, turning his head side to side. He didn't say a word. I left the office and returned to the church to meet with the elders. I told them all about the grand plan, then the elders started laying out their negative reasons why we could not build the church:

One said, "Pastor, we can't build a church like that, we have no money."

Another said, "Pastor, now I know for sure that you're a pastor and not a businessman, because that's impossible to do!"

So I met with the deacons. I presented my dream to some 600 deacons. Their negative, collective response went like this:

"Pastor! There is just no way. Where do we get that much money?"

"Pastor! Transportation is horrible. What are we going to ride to get out there?"

"Pastor! The distance from Seodaemun to Yoido is too far."

"Pastor! Not Yoido. No way!"

Next, the congregation, upon hearing my vision, opposed the plan for this reason or that reason. They stood firmly united against the idea as if they had rehearsed it, and I suffered a great deal from this unexpected strong opposition. Fortunately, there were a few who seemed optimistic about my plan; they comforted me a great deal at the time. They said:

"Pastor! This sounds like the work of God. We are in no place to say no."

"Pastor! Don't give up. God is on your side. I'm on your side."

"Pastor! I strongly agree with your idea of moving the church to Yoido."

For a long time there was a tug-of-war between the yea's and the nay's in the congregation. I didn't know what to do—I just needed to figure out a way to convince the congregation. It was then that the deaconess came to tell me about the dream she had.

When she told me about the dream, I took it as God's reaffirmation of the vision He had instilled in me. That was rejuvenating news, it got the plan moving again, for I had felt the weight of the matter on my shoulders for some time. My dream from God began to grow again—I was filled with joy.

Thinking and dreaming of all the great things God was planning to do through the newly built church, my heart filled with gladness—before this there had been many sleepless nights. I began drawing a great, awesome, picture; dreaming of some 10,000 Christians praising and worshiping God together and seeing hundreds of missionaries taking the gospel to the world.

Flying Lessons of an Eaglet

Believing in and obeying the dream from God, we broke ground to start construction in April of 1969. Twelve cranes digging at the same time left a huge hole the size of a man-made lake in the ground. Once done, they began erecting massive steel frames, for the foundation of the building. The beginning phase of the construction seemed to flow smoothly but, in retrospect, that was only the starting point for all the upcoming problems.

One of the first problems was money—and we did not have any. "Oh God," I said, "look at these bills! How am I going to pay for all this? How?" A short time after the construction began, we had used up all the money at our disposal. The bills we owed the construction company were piling up. We really needed more than $2,000,000 to build the church in Yoido, and we started with just $1,000. The cost of the construction looked as high as Mount Everest; I felt like a shocked little rabbit having to climb this huge mountain before it. I couldn't sleep—I worried constantly about where to get the money to finance the project. I couldn't do anything else but pray, and go before God with a desperate heart.

The wind and the sandstorms rising from the sand in Yoido were strong and vicious, but the lack of money was worse, it was more than I could bear. The congregation got behind the project and offered their contributions, but we were way too short. I was at the end of my rope, and didn't know what to do. I had no idea at the time that God was testing our faith. Then over the horizon came a most tempting offer. An acquaintance of mine came to me with great news. "Pastor," he said, "did you read the newspaper? An apartment complex is going to be built on Yoido!"

"Really?" I said, "An apartment complex?"

"Yes, that's right!" he said. "What do you think about building high rise apartment buildings here? We can make some money with that. I'm certain we can make a profit by selling off the apartments we build."

"Are you saying that we should put off the construction of the church and build apartments instead and make money by selling them?"

"Yes!" he said, "And I'm only saying that because you're struggling with money right now, and if we use the profits from selling the apartments things won't be as difficult as they are right now."

His idea wasn't bad. And if I went ahead with this plan we wouldn't have to worry about the money to build the church. *What should I do in this situation?* I said to myself. Build the church God has shown me, or build the apartment buildings? I decided to go with the plan that seemed more practical, rather than the plan of God. Unfortunately, that decision only led to more problems—much bigger problems.

The idea of putting off God's sanctuary to build apartments made me feel uneasy, but I thought it was the right thing to do to prepare for the construction. After putting the church construction on hold, high rise apartment buildings began to rise—first floor, second, third, they went up quickly. And, as expected, as soon as the apartments were ready, people started moving in. But less than 10 percent of the apartments were sold. The area just wasn't attractive to apartment buyers because of the poor infrastructure in Yoido at the time. Eventually the idea

The apartment complex behind the Yoido church.

of making money from selling apartments went down the drain. I had built apartments that no one wanted to live in.

The story doesn't end here though. Because we had put our money up front to build the apartments, we no longer had any money to continue the construction of the church building. With the hold on construction of the church running longer than expected, the rust on the metal frames began washing off in the rain and discoloring the ground. That combined with the heaps of lumber and other construction materials scattered all over the area gave it the appearance of a dump site.

"God's holy church site is becoming a dump site," I said to myself. "This is all my fault. I didn't follow the dream God gave me. Instead, I fell for human planning, for man's way of doing things." I went to God to ask forgiveness. "God," I said, "I'm so sorry. I've done wrong. Please forgive me. I was foolish and I did not follow your leading."

But nothing changed, and it seemed that there was no good end in sight. Every time I looked at the pitiful site I felt overburdened by it all. I ached spirit, soul, and body, and my heart was torn within me. I cried out to God each night while clinging onto the rusted frames of the foundation. I didn't know what else to do. I prayed and prayed: "God, My Father! Let your dream come to fruition. Lord, help me!" I prayed every night, all night, and sought God's mercy. "What am I supposed to do? Where do I stand? What am I supposed to do with the building project?" Finally in desperation I said, "You know what? Why don't you destroy it and let the debris kill me—just bury me in the debris!" I put my life on the line.

Whenever it rained or snowed I just sat on a bale of straw on the concrete floor and cried out to God. My heart was filled with fear. I saw the ghost town-like building site and my heart felt heavy. "What do I do now?" I said to myself. Then gradually the way I was feeling began to change. I felt God consoling me, and my heart filled with the dream again. So I decided to reassess the situation through the eyes of faith. The dream of seeing 10,000 of God's chosen people, worshipping together in a new sanctuary, began to move and grow again and the rain and the snow watered it. Then, one day, God spoke to me and said, *"Offer me what you own."*

The Yoido church sanctuary under construction.

"Lord, what do you mean?" I asked. "The only thing I own is my house. Lord, you don't mean my house, do you? You know how long and hard I worked for that house. You of all people should know that. Not the house, Lord, I can't give up the house!"

I heard His voice again, saying, *"Sell your house and offer it in faith."*

When I protested again, He said firmly, *"Yonggi, if you truly want to witness one of my miracles, won't you let go of your things first?"*

"Oh yes, Lord!" I said. "My house was yours to begin with. I'll give it back to you."

I decided to offer up my house to God in gladness and to become a witness of His miracles. That evening, I cautiously brought up the matter to my wife. "Honey, what do you think about selling the house and offering the money to God?

"What?" she exclaimed loudly. "Sell our house? No!" Then she was speechless. She did not speak that evening or the following evening or for the rest of the week. She pondered and pondered her decision until her eyes were bloodshot. It was not an easy decision to make, but the Holy Spirit was moving within her heart. At the end of the week she came to me and said: "I can no longer do this. I just cannot resist what the Holy Spirit wants. When I pray or just close my eyes, my heart gets filled with gladness and the desire to give the house to God. So we will offer this house to God in faith."

We sold the house and made an offering with the money we received for it and moved to the seventh floor of an apartment building we had put up, even though it was still undergoing construction. The day we moved in, my wife said, "We have no electricity and must draw water from the first floor. The winter season is just around the corner, and we have no heating. I'm worried about this because of the kids."

"Let's not worry," I said. "We are doing God's work first, and I am sure He will provide."

It rained softly on the day we moved, and the vast expanse of plain in Yoido was like an open desert and quite cold. We were moving into an unfinished apartment with no heat. But before we could get our things into the apartment, the building manager stopped us saying, "Pastor Cho, where do you think you are going? You need to pay first before you can move in. We need the money." And then he told his helpers to take all our things and put them out in the street.

We were very confused and puzzled by all this. I prayed as fast and earnestly as I could. "God! Help us. Holy Spirit, what am I supposed to do? Show me the way. I should be setting a good example to those people." Then I said to the manager, "I'm sorry I have not paid the money yet. But tell me who would move to a place like this with no electricity and water. If I move in and get settled, I am sure other people will hear about it and change their mind about moving in. Then when they move in you can collect your money from them and from us."

I was able to convince the manager to let us stay, and we moved our things back into the apartment. But every evening we had to fight the cold, and with no food, things looked pretty bleak. Also, when I looked down at the construction site of the church from the apartment's top floor, it hurt me even more. It seemed as though the rusted steel frame left open and barren was begging to be covered with wood and concrete. Building God's church became harder and harder.

Eagles, the kings of the air, train their eaglets in such a way that it strengthens their wings. The eagles fly to the highest points they can fly and just drop off their eaglets. Then the eaglets flap their wings desperately to stay afloat, but with their weak, undeveloped, wings, they flap in vain, awaiting their pitiful death. Then at the moment of life or death, the parent eagle swoops up the eaglets right before hitting the ground. The eaglets find comfort in the bosom of their parent eagle but that moment's short-lived, because the eagles fly back to the highest point again and drop off their eaglets once again; thus, continuing to train them. Soon, the eaglets wings strengthen and they're able to fly on their own, becoming the kings of air themselves.

That's how God has trained me severely in my faith. The moments that I'm falling down are hard and difficult, but when God scoops me up again, I feel comforted and protected, resting in His wings. I feel complete joy and like I own the whole world.

The Crushed Bowl of a Homeless Man

It was a cold winter, and the barren steel frame of the church building stood erect on that huge, open, plain. The concrete basement floor of the building was cold, but the people from the church gathered by the thousands to fast and to pray for the church and for me saying things like:

"God! Help us; help our church!"

"God! Remember our Pastor; give him strength!"

"God! Help us realize our dream of building the church!"

Finally, God began to move. He had heard our desperate pleas. A woman from the congregation sold her long hair to a wig shop and give the money as an offering. I was deeply moved by her gesture. Then during a service one day an eighty year old lady approached me in tears. She handed me something that was wrapped in newspaper and said, "Pastor! I want to help. But I have no money. All I have is this bowl and a spoon. I want to offer these to God."

"If this is the only bowl and spoon you have, how are you going to eat afterwards? I cannot accept them." I said.

"It is all right," she replied, "I can place the rice and other food on a strawboard and use my fingers to eat." I was deeply moved and hurt at the same time. "Would God not accept these worthless things from me?" she asked. "I know these will not help or mean much, but I really want to offer something to God."

Just then a businessman from the congregation rose up and said, "Pastor, I'll buy those from you." He then paid the church $12,000 for the old woman's rice bowl and spoon. Whenever I think back to those days, I still think about that old woman and long to see her. That was a breakthrough event that changed the course of the church construction. God's calculations—unfathomable from human thinking—awaited us.

One of the deacons called to me, "Pastor, look at this! I found a crushed bowl inside the offering basket."

"Who would do such a thing?" I said.

"Ah," he said, "I think I know who did it. I saw a homeless person walking onto the construction site with a gunny sack. I think he was just looking for a place to keep warm. He probably dropped it in."

I didn't know what to say. "Should I throw it away, Pastor?" the deacon asked.

"No," I said, "God accepted the two coins offered from a woman's entire possessions. How can I discard such a precious offering? Just hang onto it." My eyes filled with tears as I thought about it. The homeless person, looking to stay warm, had probably just walked in and, seeing the people earnestly praying and giving their offerings in the basket, he became deeply moved by it all and decided to give something, too. He offered his rice bowl, because he had nothing else to offer—but now I didn't know what to do with it.

The crushed rice bowl lingered in my head for some reason. Then one day a missionary leaving for his sabbatical to the United States dropped by to pay a visit before he left for the airport. "Pastor Cho," he said. "I wanted to see you before I left to tell you to be encouraged. God will provide." Then he saw the crushed rice bowl on the bookshelf beside my desk. "What is that?" he asked.

I told the missionary everything that happened at the church service. He said, "Pastor, would you let me have this rice bowl? It's a precious gift."

I gave it to him, and the missionary left on his sabbatical with the crushed rice bowl in his hand. A month later, a package arrived from Hawaii. Inside the package was a letter and a check from the Chase-Manhattan bank. After reading the letter, I was shocked and amazed, and I wept as I thanked the Lord. "Thank you, God. You're amazing. Thank you, God. I praise your name. Halleluiah!" This is what the letter said:

Greetings, Pastor,

My name is Peter Park. I own a large farm in Hawaii. I immigrated to Hawaii from Korea in 1910. I worked diligently in the sugar cane fields, and now own my own farm; it is my life's work. My children are all grown now and successful.

Respectable Pastor! I'm now seventy-two years old, and the more I age, the more I think about the country I left behind sixty years ago. I've been thinking about doing something for the country of my birth before I die. One day I met a missionary who had completed his six years of mission work in Korea, and after finding out where I was from, he started telling me about Korea. My eyes filled with tears as I listened to his stories. He also told me about Pastor Yonggi Cho of the Central Full Gospel Church, and then showed me the crushed rice bowl he brought from your church in Korea.

When I saw the rice bowl, I was deeply touched and filled with inspiration, so I too decided to give an offering to build God's church. Please accept this small token of my appreciation. Please use the $50,000 toward the building of the church. Once it is built, I'd like to come for a visit.

Sincerely,

Peter Park

That crushed rice bowl flew over the Pacific Ocean to Hawaii and then returned as $50,000. With the seemingly insignificant and petty thing that had been offered to Him, God magnified its worth and used it for His purpose. These are God's calculations—unfathomable in man's thinking.

The World's Largest Church

When I told them of this miracle through God's hands, the church members were recharged and enthused. They devoted themselves to the building project of the church. Some members sold their expensive apartment buildings and moved to the apartments that were still undergoing construction in Yoido, near the church. A young couple gave their year's salary as an offering. Everyone was united in prayer like a family. We all started dreaming of the world's largest church once again. Smiles lit up the faces of our members—it was very contagious.

One time during our building process, I went to a bank and met with its manager to borrow some money. We owed $20,000 and it had to be paid back by the end of the month. I checked all our resources, but no feasible solution was available. I entered the bank at 5:00 P.M., an hour before it closed. I had been praying about it, and the Holy Spirit gave me an idea. I was convicted to go and meet with the branch manager to borrow that sum of money. "Holy Spirit," I said, "they will think I must be crazy. I don't even have any papers ready—they will not accept my request." I was very concerned about what they would think of me.

The Holy Spirit said to me, *"My ways are far beyond human thinking. Just go and do as I said."*

So I obeyed; I rushed to the bank. I got there all right but did not know how I could meet the branch manager; and to make matters worse, there was a long line of people waiting to meet him. "What do I do, Holy Spirit? Help me."

"You're a child of God the King," He said. *"Act noble."* Hearing those words, I walked into the office of the branch manager as if I was a wealthy man.

His secretary stopped me. "Excuse me? Do you have an appointment?" she asked.

"I was sent by the most respected and important person there is," I said.

Of course I was speaking figuratively about God, but the lady apparently understood it to mean that I was sent by a person holding a high government position, because she let me in immediately, even allowing me to go ahead of others who were waiting in line. I was encouraged knowing that the Holy Spirit was with me. The branch manager greeted me with a bright smile and said, "How are you, sir? I'm sorry, but who did you say you work for?"

"Sir, I'm here with a grand plan," I said boldly. "If you do as I say, you won't be disappointed. In fact, if you meet my request I can bring you 10,000 new accounts by the first month of the year."

"Did you say 10,000 new accounts?" He looked dumbfounded.

"Yes, sir," I said, and then told him, "My name is Yonggi Cho. I'm the pastor of the largest church in Korea. There are 10,000 members in my congregation. I can have all of them transfer their accounts to your bank if you will do me this favor."

"What favor is that?" he asked.

"Lend me $20,000," I replied, and then said boldly, "I'm a businessman sent by my God, the King. I know that in the business world credibility is everything. You are a businessman, too; and you lend people money. I would like you to lend me the money. I'm in no position to file any papers, so you will just have to place your trust in me and lend me the money."

Services held in the unfinished sanctuary.

The branch manager looked greatly perplexed, so I spoke even bolder, "If you can't do it, then I'll go elsewhere."

The branch manager just kept shaking his head from side to side, and then he said, "You're quite something else, Pastor! I've never felt this kind of feeling before in my life, but your faith has convinced me, and you seem like a man who will keep his word, so okay, I'll lend you the money." Thus the Holy Spirit resolved the issue before the bank closed that day; and as promised, all the members of the church transferred their accounts to that bank.

God's hand moved amazingly to get the church construction back into operation. Every member of the congregation was committed to it with love and prayers. Finally the church building was complete, the first ever church to seat 10,000 people in one service.

During the construction many people had voiced concerns. They said things like, "A building constructed on sand will surely cave in; the infrastructure in the city is bad; the building project itself is too grand to be realized." But the dream that was lifted up to God was finally realized in four years on September 23, 1973. God kept His word. With 18,000 packed into the new sanctuary, we had a service of thanksgiving and praise to Him. All of the $2,000,000 it cost to construct the building was provided by Him.

The same year the new church was built, we also built a prayer retreat center called "Osanri Choi, Jasil Fasting Prayer Mountain"—now called "Osanri Fasting Prayer Mountain," where numerous people go to cry out to God to receive His peace.

The Rapid Growth of Yoido Church

Once the church was built, many people flocked to the new church building, marking the beginning of its era of service. By the year 1979, the congregation had grown to 100,000. By God's grace, we were experiencing a phenomenal growth. By 1981, the number doubled to 200,000, marking one of the most unprecedented growths in history.

In 1984, when we changed the name of the church from "Central Full Gospel Church" to "Yoido Full Gospel Church," we had 400,000 registered members. From seven in the morning till nine at night, a total of seven fully-packed services were carried out in the sanctuary. The congregation had outgrown the size of the church, so we had to expand. The current main sanctuary of the Yoido Full Gospel Church is the new extension that we had to install to accommodate the growth. I also had plans to build a new town around the church. We've installed two new buildings—the Educational Center and the Mission Center—all accomplished by God and dreaming a new dream, and it has all been done to show God's wondrous work. The cell groups played a great role in helping this to happen, also.

Osanri Fasting Prayer Mountain.

Numerous people go to Prayer Mountain to cry out to God to receive His peace.

A Story of Phenomenal Growth

Let us return in our story to June 1980 so that I can tell how phenomenal growth took place in our church. At that time, there were 120,000 members in the church and 8,000 cell groups. Just six months prior, we had set a goal of 30,000 new members. Our membership grew to 120,000 from 100,000, achieving two thirds growth from the current membership count. So in 1980, we set a goal for 150,000, and I instructed all the cell group members to reach out to one household in their neighborhoods for the remainder of the year. According to my new mandate, it meant that the existing 8,000 cell groups needed to witness to 8,000 more households by the end of the year. If we consider four people as making up the average household, it meant bringing in 32,000 new members to the church.

That clearly demonstrates amazing growth. To achieve that, the church did not need to advertise, extort, or even put out commercials. As pastor, I just needed to exhort and motivate the cell group leaders, and keep the new goal of 32,000 new member in their minds, and help them to accomplish it by sending out printed visual reminders saying, "Each household in the cell groups needs to witness to one other household. That won't be difficult to do." To do this, each cell group selected one non-believing household and began to pray for them and witness to them. This boosted many cell group members' confidence in reaching out to non-believers and showed them how easy it was to lead others to Christ. Some even reached out to two or three households. All their efforts culminated in massive growth at the church, and we ended the year 1980 with 150,000 members and 10,000 cell groups.

Now not all goals are always achieved. But in terms of church growth, everything hinges on whether or not the church sets goals; this is an absolute necessity. Only those churches that set goals will see growth.

In 1981, we became more ambitious for the Lord and raised our goals of reaching out from one household to four households. Such an endeavor meant leading 80,000 new members to the church in the first half of the year and another 80,000 in the latter half. At the end of the year, there were 310,000 members in the church. Utilizing the cell groups, the church experienced growth again in 1984 without TV advertising or mass communication. Instead, by word of mouth and one-on-one contact, we reached the goal of having 500,000 members.

There is no such thing as stunted growth for a living and active organization in the context of church growth. Too many churches grow to about 500 to 1,000 members and come to a standstill. Members of such churches come to believe that there are no other lost souls to reach, and even the pastors become complacent and gradually forget their treasured vision of spreading the gospel to the ends of the earth—or at least throughout their surrounding communities. They do not seem to know that the working of the Holy Spirit within their church diminishes with stagnant growth.

After many years, the Yoido Full Gospel Church stands tall with 780,000 members. And we still experience the working of the Holy Spirit in every part of our church. According to some statistics, it only takes five minutes to fill up the 12,000 seating capacity of the new sanctuary on any given Sunday for a 9:00 A.M. service. And for the members to exit the facility only takes ten minutes. Isn't this amazing? The Yoido Full Gospel Church made the Guinness Book of Records in 2005 as the largest church in the world. It has now become a tourist attraction, a "must-see" during a trip to Korea. I have been just following God's lead, taking the dream He gave me to the world. And God did all this! He's still moving and working, and I'm still dreaming and following His lead.

Yoido Full Gospel Church — the largest church congregation in the world.

One of the Sunday morning services.

Dr. Cho speaking at an international conference.

Part 5

A Ministry That Extends Out to the World

Open Your Mouth Wide and I Will Fill It
I had lunch with a renowned neurosurgeon one morning. He was a well-known authoritative figure in the field. He told me about various discoveries made in the field of neurosurgery. "Pastor, did you know that the speech area nerve controls all other nerves in the brain?"

"Yes, I knew that long ago," I said, laughing.

"Really? How did you know that?" he asked. "They just recently discovered it."

I said, "I heard it from Dr. James."

"Who is Dr. James?" he asked.

I said, "He was a renowned figure during the apostolic era, some 2,000 years ago. In his book, the Book of James, he goes into a lengthy discussion about the importance of the behaviors of tongue and speech."

"Does the Bible really discuss such things?" he asked, obviously surprised.

"Absolutely," I said. "If you look at James 3:1-5, it is clearly recorded that those who control their tongue can control their body."

"Really?" he said. "That's exactly what I report in my paper. The speech area nerve that allows humans to speak has the power to control other parts of the body."

The doctor then went into great details about that. Let me give you some examples of what he said.

"If a person says, 'I am gradually getting weaker,' other nerves in the body immediately receive that command from the speech area nerve and obey it, saying something like, 'Let's get weak, we need to get weaker, that's the message from the command tower.' That is how a person gets weak and becomes ill. In other words, those nerves can weaken an individual.

"If another person says, 'I am not capable. I cannot do this,' then all the nerves in his body respond accordingly, almost as if they say to each other, 'We are not capable; that is what the speech area nerve commanded; that is an order; we need to prepare to become incompetent, we must give up all means of utilizing our capabilities.'

"And if someone else says, 'I am too old; I am too tired to do anything else,' the speech area nerve will exercise its power and take command over all the nerves. The nerves will then respond as if they were saying, 'Yes, we are all old. Let's prepare to die—to rest in the grave.'

"But if an individual says, 'I'm healthy,' then the speech area nerve sends its command to other nerves, effectively saying, 'You're all healthy.' They respond, 'We're all healthy, very healthy.' They then process the command and become healthy. That way even sick people can regain their health.

"Therefore, Pastor, if a person changes the way he speaks, he also changes holistically—because all parts of our body work together."

After hearing the doctor, I reaffirmed the importance of words and at our next service told the congregation: "We need to use words correctly. If you say things like, 'It is so hot I am going to die of this heat; I am so full if I take another bite I am going to die; I like that so much I am going to die; I am so scared I am going to die,' then you may very well see death. From now on, let us change those death-ridden expressions that we too often use to a more Biblical expression, 'I am going to live for Jesus Christ,' and then I'm sure you will see differences in yourselves." I explained strongly to the congregation how important it is to speak God's Word through our mouths, and how that leads to living a successful life.

Years before, I had also learned that the Holy Spirit desires His people to use language creatively. I recall this from back in the early days of my ministry, while preaching, I felt and heard the Holy Spirit speaking this to me: *"I want to heal people, but if you don't communicate this message through your mouth, no healing will take place. Listen to my words! From the beginning of creation there was light when I said, 'Let there be light!' That came true, because that is what I proclaimed. From now on just keep proclaiming, 'Be healed in the name of Jesus Christ.' Proclaim through your messages that God's Word and the Holy Spirit will be with us, and it shall come to pass."*

God wanted me to proclaim with my mouth that He had healed those illnesses. But I was too afraid. What if nothing happened after I proclaimed such a thing? What would people say? So I told God, "God, I'm afraid. But I will do as you tell me. I'll start with the less serious illnesses first." After that, whenever I preached, the Holy Spirit would tell me that a cripple had been healed, or a cancer patient had been healed, but I denied such convictions and, instead, I proclaimed only the minor illnesses.

One day during a service I felt impelled to say, "Someone here with a migraine has been healed." I hardly finished saying the words when a person got healed immediately. I was amazed at what God was doing through me. But I was also encouraged, and I began accepting the healings to be the work of the Holy Spirit who resides in me and proclaimed it even more. "A deaf person has been healed in the name of Jesus. Hallelujah!" "A cancer has left a person's body in the name of Jesus. Hallelujah!" I claimed God's Word boldly and the congregation began experiencing healings. Realizing that my words echoed as I spoke them in that large sanctuary, I spoke them even more loudly and boldly with my mouth wide open.

In 1991, God said there would be 700,000 members in our church. So I proclaimed it to the congregation. "Our congregation will grow to 700,000 members, for there is going to be a great revival. I believe it, and I affirm it through the eyes of my faith. It shall come to pass."

As a result, our congregation grew to 700,000 and beyond— to 780,000, all worshipping God together. If someone should ask, "How does one lead a ministry in such a joyful mood and with courage?" I would respond like this: "Change the way you speak. Unleash creative words—the language of the Holy Spirit speaking through a vessel of faith. He'll do the rest."

The Holy Spirit: the Owner of our Mission Ministries

The Holy Spirit is the owner of our church's mission work. All I have done is follow His lead, proclaim what He says, and obey what He has instilled in my heart. From the beginning of our church, God had me dreaming to take the gospel through world missions to the nations and to the people who did not know God. I believed it and boldly proclaimed it with my mouth in front of people. For this very purpose, I began studying English, which is a worldwide language. Since I did not have time to attend an institute, I studied vocabulary and practiced English conversation. My goal was to be able to preach in English that could be understood by native speakers. I worked very hard to achieve this.

Then in September of 1964, God used me for this very purpose—mission ministry, something I had been proclaiming with my mouth. From that time I became a microphone of the gospel to the world with God's help. At first, traveling to these different places and meeting the people was satisfying enough. Then I became driven with a mission to carry the gospel to the world. I suffered a great deal from so much travel—jet lag, having to adapt to different food and a sleep pattern that often made me sick. But God was always with me, so I was greatly comforted. Those troubles didn't slow me down. Seeing those people reaching out to God upon hearing my messages was beyond any joy I had known. Forty years have now passed since I began taking the gospel to the world. Someone told me that according to his calculations I had traveled one hundred fourteen times around the world. God lavished His grace upon me, just as I had proclaimed.

Almost ten years later, just about the time of the completion of the Yoido Full Gospel Church building, the Holy Spirit spoke to my heart to prepare five hundred missionaries to take God's gospel out to the world. Once the church building was completed, I believed and proclaimed what God had shown me through dreams concerning world missions. In only a short time we were able to build a world outreach mission center, the first ever in Korea, and begin sending out missionaries wherever the gospel was needed. Some forty years later, there are 780 missionaries from our church serving throughout the world. God has certainly blessed this ministry. All this we were able to accomplish through the working of the Holy Spirit.

CGI (Church Growth International)

Since 1964, the year I was invited to a general assembly meeting of the Assemblies of God in Springfield, Missouri, I have been speaking adamantly about our church growth principles to pastors, ministry leaders, and the laity in churches around the world. I strongly emphasize church growth principles through cell group organization. God erected the world's largest church on the Island of Yoido in South Korea, and uses me to tell what He has done and what it looks like.

In spite of my weakness due to illnesses, 1964 was the year I began traveling the world, and from 1964 to 1973 I traveled at least three times a year to Japan, the Philippines, and Taiwan to speak at various functions. Everywhere I went, the Holy Spirit worked powerfully through me, and the churches around the world began to pay attention. The principles at work in what was then Central Full Gospel Church challenged churches around the world to do the same for God. After our church moved to Yoido from Seodae Gate in 1973, we started becoming well known and receiving publicity. Billy Graham came to Seoul in 1973 to hold his Crusade, and that same year, we held the World's Pentecostal Church Conference at our church. The following year, Campus Crusade for Christ hosted a grand conference that sparked the beginning of a revival in South Korea. It was God's elaborate plan for our church to be planted in Yoido.

Crusade at Olympic Stadium in Seoul with Robert Schuller.

While these grand, international Christian events were being held in Seoul, our church stepped up to meet the demands and challenges for hosting and supporting those events. We offered our church as the venue for these functions and served as a wonderful working model of the manifestation of revivals breaking out in South Korean churches, being located near the renowned Yoido Plaza was also an added advantage. After that, invitations began pouring in from America, Europe, Australia and Southeast Asian countries for me to come to speak about church growth.

In 1973, I spent about six months abroad. Most invitations came from European countries, so I was able to travel to churches in West Germany, France, Switzerland, Norway, Denmark, Sweden, England, Italy and Portugal. Even in those demanding times, I was still able to write and publish books that became bestsellers in West Germany, Sweden, and Finland.

Through revival gatherings, conferences and published books, I began to draw more attention from Europe. God's keys on church growth took on wings and flew out to the world.

A Million Dollar Answer to Prayer

One day in 1976, I was on a Lufthansa flight heading back to South Korea after completing a grand revival gathering and seminars in Germany. Sitting in the cabin, I prayed and thanked God for allowing the meetings to go so well, and felt an intimate fellowship with the Holy Spirit. At that moment, I felt a strong sense of vision come over me. The Holy Spirit then spoke to me in a soft voice: *"I want you to build an international training center big enough to house pastors from churches around the world. You are traveling everywhere around the world with an urgent message for my Body, but I want the number of pastors and faithful servants hearing the message to increase many fold. The best way for them to hear the message is to have them come to Seoul to see with their own eyes what you are doing in your ministry. Build the center. Provide a place for them to come and see what goes on in the church. It is the best way to rekindle their passion to spread the gospel and apply the principles you are teaching them."*

I was dumbfounded. I didn't know what to make of what He said. I replied, "Lord, how am I supposed to do this? I am from a Third World country. From our Western brother's perspective, South Korea is the mission field. Without a doubt, such a center should be built in America or in Europe." But the thought did not leave me. It burned into my heart and the urge to take on the project intensified.

When I got back in Korea, I prayed to find God's lead; I searched for His way. Like Gideon, I finally decided to spread out the wool before Him and prayed to Him, saying, "Lord, if this plan is indeed yours, I need you to show me. I will conduct a one-time offering collection at the church and if the amount needed to complete this project is collected through that offering, I'll take that as a sign that you approve of it."

I sat with the elder board and discussed the plan from God. The elders responded rather dubiously to my message. We agreed to announce the plan the following Sunday and said that we needed $1,000,000 to build this center. Whether it's a spontaneous collection of offering or an allotted offering, making such an announcement is not easy. Quite frankly, I was afraid that the congregation might not make any offering for the cause. I prayed, "Heavenly Father, if this is your will, give us one million dollars. If you don't, then I'll take that as a no."

Sunday finally arrived. After the sermon, I disclosed the plan of building a mission center and how it would be used and asked for offerings for its construction. We collected the money, and the head of the finance committee told us the total of the offering. Amazingly, it was exactly one million dollars.

Search for a Ministry Partner

We began building the international mission center, which we named Church Growth International (CGI), adjacent to the Yoido Full Gospel Church building. During its construction, I had to hire a new staff to carry on the ministry. Just as we fine-tuned the vision, mission statement, and the capacity of this new ministry, I realized this was something that I would not be able to do along with all of my other responsibilities. I knew I had to put someone else in charge.

The name John Hurston came quickly to my mind. Missionary Hurston, a servant of God, had shared the ministry with me from the days we were in the slum area of Seoul, when we had a small tent church in Bulgwang-dong. He played an important role in erecting the church in Seodae Gate. Before departing to Vietnam in 1969, he was my ministry partner and brother in the Lord for ten years. During the Vietnam War,

Missionary Hurston planted several churches, but in 1975 he had to flee when the Communist Vietcong seized southern Vietnam.

I found John in Pasadena, California. When I arrived, I discovered that John was recuperating from a heart disorder caused by a minor heart attack. He looked very fatigued, and since I last saw him five years earlier he had aged even more years than that.

"John," I said, "it will be all right. God will give you strength."

"Pastor Cho," he replied, "leaving Vietnam was the most bitter experience of my life. I spent nearly six years planting those churches in Vietnam, and when I had to leave I cried for days. At that time I had no other choice."

"Do you have any plans for now?" I asked.

"I don't know," he said. "The Assemblies of God requested that I go to Taiwan as a missions director but I honestly don't feel up to it."

I explained to John the vision I had received from God and how He had provided the funds to build it, and then I said to him, "I believe I need to find someone who can lead this new ministry and you're the person I'm thinking of."

John paused to think for a moment. He was interested, so we prayed together. When we finished, he said, "Very well, I believe God wants me to lead that ministry."

"I think so too," I said happily. "Praise God!"

Then John said, "But if He wants me to serve Him through that ministry, He needs to do something about my heart condition."

Lay Minister Choi was scheduled to speak at a gathering in Los Angeles the following month. At that assembly, she laid her hands on John, and he had a feeling of an immediate and affirmative healing go through him. Some time after that, the Reverend John Hurston was on his way to South Korea to become my ministry partner once again.

Immanence of Church Growth Era

Another incident confirmed that God would enable me to build CGI. We desperately needed an international advisory committee to assess the needs of numerous pastors around the world so that we could build a facility that would provide ample resources to these pastors. After we built the World Mission Center in November 1976, I began searching for potential committee members. In February of the following year, I invited twenty-four pastors to a meeting at a hotel in North Hollywood, California. At that meeting, I explained my vision from the Lord of using different organizational methods to spread church growth principles around the world. I emphasized the urgent need to share our knowledge with the churches in Third World countries. I told the attendees how we needed to strengthen those churches and encourage them to grow so that they could witness the gospel throughout the world. The pastors were quite enthusiastic about my vision.

When we decided to elect a chairperson, they all insisted and unanimously elected me. All the attendees agreed to support me faithfully in establishing CGI meetings, not only in South Korea and the United States but around the world as well. I strongly felt that CGI was the tangible embodiment of the expressed needs of the churches of the 1980s. If the 1960s

Dr. Cho laying hands on a woman at a crusade held in Honduras.

was the decade of recovery for the planting and spreading of the church movement, and the 1970s the era of outpouring of miracles and healing, then the 1980s surely affirmed the era of church growth. If the healing and miracle movement did not contribute to the growth of churches, then it would not have been useful to the churches that embraced it. As a matter of fact, all spiritual miracles from the Holy Spirit were given to the believers in order to establish the Body of Christ. And they don't just symbolize spiritual encouragement but physical growth of the Body as well, so in that respect church growth is indeed the will of God.

Church growth in the context of the Body of Christ and its future is of grave importance; therefore, we must be serious when dealing with this topic. Church growth isn't just some temporary fad. Jesus came to establish His Church, but that Church has been dormant. Now is the time for her to wake up. Churches that wake up will grow.

A Love Letter from Our Church

All the blessings we've received are not only for us to keep. The reason for God's pouring out of all these blessings, love, and grace is to serve our neighbors—those in need. I've been thinking about how to share God's love and blessings with the world. After much pondering, I've decided to do the following:

First, our church must carry out the teaching of "Loving our neighbors like ourselves." I realized we can do much just by showing a little interest in our neighbors, so our members were asked to bring in recycled paper and newspapers. We then sold the papers and with the money we used to help children with heart disease who desperately needed surgery. This outreach has become a tradition of our church. So far, we've helped around 3,000 children. These children are doing well, living their new lives birthed through the love that we all shared.

In 1992, we started collecting milk cartons, old clothes, and coins found lying around the house. All these efforts went to helping those in financial need. The old clothes were sent to countries like Angola, Papua, New Guinea, and countries ravaged and devastated by internal wars.

In 1999, we founded a new outreach ministry known as "Good People." Its purpose was to share the light of Christ by offering financial assistance and service to those in need domestically and abroad. Good People formed international relief groups to go out to countries like India, Pakistan, Sri Lanka, Bangladesh, China, Kenya, and others—crossing all racial boundaries. Their task was to provide the hope and light of Jesus Christ by comforting physically and emotionally those who were hurt by internal wars, natural disasters, and earthquakes. We are also helping North Korean defectors to adapt to the life style in South Korea, as well as sharing the gospel with them.

The church is striving to offer warmth and love to our neighbors, hoping to raise up little "homes of hope" in their hearts.

Do you know what our national religion is—it is Buddhism. Non-Christian Koreans, for whatever reason, but likely because they lack knowledge about Christianity, harshly criticize Christianity in every way they can. Therefore, I thought long and hard about ways to spread the gospel effectively, especially to these non-Christian Koreans.

Herald of the Gospel: *Kookmin-Ilbo* (newspaper)

First, we established *Kookmin-Ilbo*. Upon much pondering and prayer, God told me to establish this newspaper for the purpose of spreading the gospel. In 1988, the first edition of *Kookmin-Ilbo* was published. At first there were many obstacles to overcome. It wasn't easy to launch a new newspaper. As with every new endeavor, many voiced their opposition and criticism.

One said, "Pastor, a newspaper? What would a church do with a newspaper division? I'm against it!"

Another said, "Pastor, the budget to run a newspaper division would be astronomical. We just don't have the money for it."

There were many moments of struggle due to a shortage of financial resources. But I planted the seed of faith in them. I told them: "Let's change our way of speaking. Let's not say "can't" anymore. No matter what anyone says, we can do this! You'll see, many will come to know the light of Jesus Christ through *Kookmin-Ilbo*. Households that subscribe to and read *Kookmin-Ilbo* will hear the gospel. People out on the street will read and hear about Jesus. Just think about it. Doesn't that sound like a wonderful thing? This is the will of God. Let's give it a try!"

The seed was planted and now we are reaping its fruits. Now *Kookmin-Ilbo* is circulated worldwide and takes the gospel everywhere. It is a "missionary without voice," that has become a major messenger of the gospel.

The Internet Broadcasting Station

Second, along with *Kookmin-Ilbo* our church decided to use the Internet, the most powerful information media that has ever been developed, to take the gospel to the people. In retrospect, the unprecedented use of the Internet to share the gospel was an amazing piece of wisdom from God, because at the time no other churches had considered it. Thanks to God, I utilized various creative methods to achieve our mission to spread the gospel before the Internet was filled with secular users that spread many other things. I established FGTV (Full-Gospel Television), the first on-line Internet channel ever, and used it to deliver live worship services to homes and places where the Internet was available. It truly shocked a lot of people then.

It was God who showed me all those innovative ideas. Currently, the Internet broadcasting channel delivers the gospel in eight different languages: Korean, English, Japanese, Chinese, French, Spanish, Russian, and German. This medium allows people all over the world to experience God through worship services. When you can, please visit our church web site. Our Korean language Internet television station is at: http://fgtv. com/, with the other languages listed at the bottom of the Home page, and our English language station is at: http://english. fgtv.com/.

Elim Welfare Town

Third, the Elim Welfare Town was established and contributed to the cause of spreading the gospel. Built about the same time as the Kookmin-Ilbo Building, the Elim Welfare

Town was built to house elderly people who have no place to live and unfortunate adolescents who can not afford even the basic living needs. For the latter group, we provide a technical school so that they can learn and acquire the skills needed to obtain jobs, along with certification programs. There are other programs and activities available for its users, actively contributing to the general social welfare in small ways.

Awarded the Family of Man Medallion

In June of 2005, I received a surprising letter from the United States. It was a gift from God. I was deeply impressed by it. I cried much after I read it. This is what it said: "The Council of Churches of the City of New York is proud to present the Reverend Yonggi Cho, *The Family of Man Medallion Award.* The council recognizes your dedication and commitment to the spreading of the gospel and awards you for your efforts to travel wherever the gospel is needed. Congratulations!"

My heart pounded in excitement as I read the letter.

That's because the award was created to recognize certain people with special leadership qualities and was given to those who shared a very special love and interest for the people around the globe. The past recipients include notables like Dwight D. Eisenhower, John F. Kennedy, Richard Nixon, Jimmy Carter, John Rockefeller, Henry Ford and others. There have been

Dr. Cho receiving the Family of Man Medallion from the president of the CCCNY.

twenty-three recipients so far. It was a significant award and the fact that I received it just overwhelmed me. I was greatly honored by it. What's even more amazing is the fact that the award was last given in 1986, and I was the first recipient after a span of nineteen years. This was also the first time that a religious leader or a Korean had been honored with the award.

This was my speech at the awards ceremony: "I'm not qualified to receive this award. But I thank God and give Him all the credit, and give Him all the honor. I would also like to thank my congregation, who have supported me all these years; and, finally, my family. Receiving this award only means that I have to work even harder for God's kingdom."

All these things were possible only by God's grace. As I shared in my stories, I believe anything is possible with God. Even now, I'm still a dreamer of dreams before my holy God. "Being confident of this, that He who began a good work in you will carry it on to completion until the day of Christ Jesus" (Philippians 1:6).

A True Mission Delivers the Power of the Holy Spirit

A mission that works in harmony with the Holy Spirit is a true mission. In that light, the mission always is to deliver the power of the Holy Spirit. The first step to experiencing the power of the Holy Spirit is to acknowledge the presence of the Holy Spirit in our lives and to welcome Him into our lives. That's the first step!

Whenever I go on mission trips, I always pray the following: "Holy Spirit! Go with me. Help me to witness God's healing power to others and to bestow His blessings. I welcome you. I acknowledge you. I welcome you into my heart. Come, come, Holy Spirit!" Once I receive His anointing, I boldly claim whatever the Holy Spirit wants me to claim.

"In Jesus name, I cast out all the powers of darkness!"

"You shall be healed in the blood of Jesus flowing from the Cross."

"In Jesus name, I bless you brothers and sisters."

Amazingly, whenever I proclaim the presence of the Holy Spirit with my mouth, I bear the fruits of His healing powers and blessings regardless of wherever I may be or whomever I'm ministering to. This is the evidence of the Holy Spirit working through me.

The following incident occurred during a revival meeting I was leading a few years ago in Europe—it shows how I sometimes fight the Holy Spirit because of fear, and what happens when I obey Him. The place was packed with 1500 people that evening. I saw a lady in a wheelchair sitting in the front row. Her legs were so awkwardly positioned that it was just painful looking at them. I saw in her eyes a desire to get healed; it was so intense that I tried to look elsewhere. That is because I was not relying on God at the moment; I was thinking and relying more on my own judgment. But the Holy Spirit spoke powerfully to my heart that He wanted me to proclaim her healing. And this is how I responded: "Holy Spirit! Why did you place that woman in the front row seat? The more I look at her, the more I doubt any healing can occur; I just don't have any faith for her to be healed."

I just ignored what the Holy Spirit was saying to me and kept preaching my sermon. I dared not to make eye contact with her. But in the moments I did, I couldn't help but think these thoughts: "She's too badly injured. Lady, why are you looking at me like that? Oh, no, what if she comes up to me for the laying on of hands." Of course, I turned my head and looked elsewhere. But toward the end of my sermon, the Holy Spirit spoke to me in a more powerful way that He wanted to heal her. At that moment, I had no choice but to pay attention to what He was telling me to do: *"Go to the lady in the wheelchair and help her stand up on her feet!"*

"What?" I said, "the lady over there—sitting in the wheelchair? I am not Jesus. How can I do such a thing—look at those legs."

"Just do as I say, raise her up!" The Holy Spirit spoke very clearly to me, but I was in great fear.

"I cannot. I'm sorry, I just cannot!" I refused yet again. Instead I proclaimed God's Word to others in the place. I proclaimed it powerfully. First a blind lady was healed.

"Right now, a blind woman will receive God's healing. She'll open her eyes. In the name of Jesus, be healed!"

A woman in the audience shouted, "I can see! I can really see!"

Others there that evening received healings as I proclaimed God's healing power in the name of Jesus. I proclaimed and proclaimed, "You shall be healed in the name of Jesus!"

Then the Holy Spirit spoke to me yet again. "Step down from the pulpit and help the woman in the wheelchair to stand up!"

I pleaded with Him, "Holy Spirit, look at her. Her legs are beyond healing. I am too afraid."

His only reply was to tell me sternly, "I want you to go to her and do as I tell you!"

Dr. Cho ministers to the people.

"Okay, I'll do it. I'll obey." I finally was convicted to obey His leading.

Toward the end of the meeting, I stepped down from the pulpit and walked slowly to where she sat. I bent over slightly and whispered into her ear. "Lady, if you want to, you can get out of the wheelchair." I then quickly turned and faced the other way. It was right at that moment, that God began His miracle. I heard people clapping, and someone shouting, "Halleluiah! Halleluiah!" I quickly turned back to see. I couldn't believe my eyes. The lady got up from the wheelchair and started walking around.

"How can that be!?" I exclaimed. I just couldn't believe my eyes. I stood there with my mouth wide open in amazement. I was just completely speechless. Right then I began to feel so bad about refusing the conviction of the Holy Spirit, that my head tilted forward from shame. I just couldn't keep my head up straight, and I said to Him: "Holy Spirit, I'm sorry. Had I been obedient from the beginning, You would have been praised even more gloriously by all the people. I was foolish. I forgot how you work through me, I was not trusting you and remembering how you have worked through me. I just was not remembering that. From now on, I will obey. I will do as you say."

The Holy Spirit is a very important person to me. I can also say that He is the closest friend I have. He is my teacher, my spiritual teacher, whom I trust and rely on. He is also my partner.

Winning Spiritual Warfare

Soldiers heading out to the battlefield will do everything it takes for a victory. They prepare thoroughly for the battle, paying attention to every little detail; and if such well-prepared soldiers are matched with a strong, courageous, leader, then the battle is pretty much over—the battle is already won.

Did you know that we are all engaged in spiritual warfare? Our enemy is the devil. We are God's children, His chosen, and we march daily toward heaven. But the devil does not want that, and he will do whatever it takes to thwart us from that path, because he wants to lead us along the road to destruction. That is why we must fight the devil in spiritual warfare.

What's unique about this warfare is that it is not visible to the naked eye. There are not any weapons available that we can see with our eyes and use with our hands. By ourselves we cannot win against the devil. But, thank our God, the mighty weapon at our disposal is to serve our Commander-in-Chief, our Lord Jesus Christ. That is because He won the battle for us 2000 years ago. The victory is His, and through Him the victory is ours!

It was about 2,000 years ago that Jesus died on the Cross for our sins. To those who were there, His dying seemed as if death had swallowed Him, but He defeating death and the devil and was resurrected in three days. Through His resurrection, we received eternal life and victory over defeat. We gained health over sickness. Success over failure. That is why we are engaged in a warfare that has already been won—a sure and certain victory!

Dr. Cho speaking at an conference celebrating the 100th anniversary of the Azusa Street Revival held in Colosseum Stadium in LA.

The devil will do whatever it takes to prevent us from reaching the top where victory awaits us. He will use lies, tricks, illnesses, despair, sadness, anything he can convince us to accept. He keeps whispering into our ears, "The road to Jesus is too tough. Just give up!" He will persistently tell us, "You are too busy. You have so much studying to do. You haven't time to read the Word. You are wasting precious time by praying." The devil appeals to our natural laziness and tries to get us to stop reading the Word and praying. It's Sunday and you need to rest. You're too tired to go to church. It's okay to take time off from Jesus. The devil makes our eyes and heart turn to television, computers, and the world.

To fight off these temptations, Jesus sent the Holy Spirit. If we befriend the Holy Spirit, we won't fall for the devil's lies and traps. Instead, we will be waving the flag of victory high and proud.

For the past fifty years of my ministry, I have experienced victory doing God's work. If I had not known the Scripture, *"Come to me, all you who are weary and burdened, and I will give you rest"* (Matthew 11:28), I would not have had victory. Overseeing a congregation of 780,000 means there are weddings and funerals every day. There are often sick church members who ask me to pray for them. And there is not a day in which there are not new situations that must have my attention. It is constant warfare and constant work.

There was a time when I constantly thought and worried about our missionaries scattered out in the world, and the responsibilities of running and operating *Kookmin-Ilbo*, along with the problems of day-to-day life that sometimes nearly overwhelmed me. At times I wondered what would happen if I were to die that day, for there were days when I really felt like I was going to die from exhaustion. But then the Holy Spirit spoke this to me: *"Why do you take all these burdens upon yourself? The are too heavy for you to carry. This church is not yours, it is mine! I already know the future plans of this church. All you have to do is rest in me."* My eyes filled with tears when I heard His words. I knew then that I only had to follow His leading and just stay in constant communication with Him. Once I realized that, my life changed completely.

My day begins at 4:00 A.M. As soon as I wake up, I pray and meditate on the Word of God. That is how I begin my day. I praise Him with songs of praise, and then I go over everything He has given me to do for that day and I thank Him and ask Him to bless me and the things we will do that day together. I also pray for the spiritual warfare of Christians around the world, that there may be victory. My day begins in prayer and ends in prayer. I constantly seek His guidance, and I constantly train myself with the sword of the Word and the shield of prayer to win the spiritual battles. But the most potent weapon is obedience to the Holy Spirit. Training consistently in the guidance of the Holy Spirit is the surest way of leading us to victory.

The Holy Spirit gives me joy. He gives me strength to fight the devil and strong faith. Because of Him, my life is full of thanksgiving and victories. With the wisdom He gives me, I am able to accomplish many things. He pours His healing power through me, and by His power I witness to others and do mission work. Through His help, I was able to establish the world's largest church.

My heart is filled completely with the Holy Spirit. This is the secret of my success. I have been able to share the gospel with many people and do all things—large or small—and be successful at them because of the working of the Holy Spirit in my life. If you, also, fill your heart and your life with the Holy Spirit, you will see the wonders He will work in and through you. Even now I stand right behind Christ Jesus, proudly holding high the flag of the Cross, ready to win every spiritual battle against the devil. Jesus has already won, and from this point on I will only experience victory. I am so confident because the Holy Spirit will be with me.

Fellowship with the Holy Spirit

The secret to all of my successes is fellowship with the Holy Spirit. Communing with the Holy Spirit is the most important and central concept to all success. No matter how much time I spend preparing a message, I would be unable to bear any sort of fruit with my sermons without His anointing. And a sermon with no spiritual results would be a practice in futility.

Many people do not correctly understand what it means to have fellowship with the Holy Spirit. People consider it as being spiritually reborn, receiving the baptism of the Holy Spirit, and experiencing the power and authority of the Holy

Spirit. But that is not what it means to have fellowship with the Holy Spirit.

I myself lived with this view for a long time. In seminary my sole ambition was to receive a degree so that I could become a famous speaker. As a born-again Christian, speaking in tongues, I would openly confess that I had received the Holy Spirit baptism. I, also, told myself, "Yes, with this I am fulfilled."

God, however, changed my attitude. He showed me that the Holy Spirit may have shown His power and caused me to be born again, but He must also fill my existence with His presence as well. Therefore, to have fellowship with the Holy Spirit is to have Him actively living within you, have Him be a part of every moment of your life, and for you to be constantly aware of Him.

Before coming to this realization, my work in response to God's calling was very turbulent and unstable. Although I believed myself to be teaching commendable lessons with great results, in actuality I was struggling fruitlessly. Time passed, and in a few years I grew out of my small tent church. Sometimes I would feel that my sermon had been a great success, and I would go home full of joy. Then at other times I felt that sermon had been a complete failure. And if I did not see at least one person receive Jesus into their heart at the end of the service, I would feel a heavy depression weighing on my heart. At such times I would scream out against the Lord: "God, why do you not help me? I want every sermon to be a good sermon."

One day in the winter of 1960 I was praying alone in the church when God began to speak to my soul: *My son, if only you had fellowship with the Holy Spirit, your ministry would be doubled and you would be blessed with greater spiritual abilities.*

"Father God," I replied, "have I not already received the Holy Spirit? I have been reborn. I have received the baptism of the Holy Spirit. What more do I need?"

"Yes," He said, *"you do have the Holy Spirit in your life. However, you do not have the intimate fellowship with the Holy Spirit that you need. Think of it in terms of marriage. You might have the title of a marriage with your wife, but if you were to continue in that manner without true fellowship with her, you would eventually come to consider her not as a person but as just another object in the house, having only a secondary value."*

These words developed a new outlook upon my ministry, and I came to have a genuine fellowship with the Holy Spirit. Before I heard the words of the Lord, I realized my fellowship was as it is described in 1 John 1:3, "We proclaim to you what we have seen and heard, so that you also may have fellowship with us. And our fellowship is with the Father and with His Son, Jesus Christ."

Just as most Christians, I felt I was in fellowship with God the Father and Jesus. I prayed to the Father, and I prayed to Jesus. I held services for the Father and I held services for the Son. I referred to the Father and I referred to the Son, but seldom did I mention the Holy Spirit.

As I studied the Bible, however, I came to realize that not only does it instruct us to have fellowship with the Son and the Father, who are one and the same, but also to have fellowship and dialogue with the Holy Spirit (Philippians 2:1; see also Acts 13:2). God the Father revealed His power and performed wonders throughout the course of the Old Testament, after which He sent Jesus Christ, who died on the Cross, rose again, and ascended into heaven. Christ Jesus now sits at the right hand of God. Yet as Jesus ascended into heaven, He promised that He would send the Holy Spirit in His place (John 15:26, 16:7).

I always recognize the presence of the Holy Spirit and invite Him in when we hold a service. The reason I do this is because the Holy Spirit is a definite person in and of himself. Before going to speak the message I always speak the following confession: "Holy Spirit, I believe in you, I welcome you, and I love you. I depend on you. Holy Spirit, let us go forth together. Let us reveal to the congregation the glory of God."

As I begin my sermon, I pray once again within my heart: "Holy Spirit, I begin my sermon now. As you provide the knowledge, wisdom, and understanding, I will pass it on to the congregation."

As the sermon comes to an end, I sit and pray once more: "Holy Spirit, we have just accomplished a wonderful thing. Is this not so? Glory be to God. All glory be to you alone."

Once I started depending on the Holy Spirit in this manner, I felt the anointing of the Lord on my life and my ministry. Not only did I feel His healing power, I also saw many newborn Christians brought forth. My life has become a boat sailing atop the waves of the Holy Spirit.

God is Primary, Family Secondary

I wish to explain the importance of fellowship with the Holy Spirit with illustrations from my own life. Traveling back in time to when I had just gotten married, I wanted to become a famous evangelist, and I worked hard to achieve that goal. I wanted to be the Korean Billy Graham. In those days, I very much wanted to be the type of pastor that served with the single purpose of serving the Lord.

Birthday party of Dr.Cho's wife.

I brought my wife home after the wedding. A week passed before I started preparing myself for a busy life of evangelical sermons. My routine consisted of having a service and giving my sermon in one church, after which I would immediately go out and give a sermon elsewhere. I only came home on the weekends so that I could give my wife the laundry. Six months passed in this manner, and as time passed I became increasingly fired up with the ambition of becoming a strong evangelist.

For a time my wife remained the very picture of kindness. When I would come home from an evangelical gathering, she would run to the door to greet me. She loved me dearly and would diligently prepare my meals. As time passed, however, and my work habits remained unchanged, my wife started becoming affected. She no longer seemed excited to see me, and occasionally tears would start streaming from her face. It was at that point that I began to realize that there was a problem. Because it was still early in our marriage, my wife was still extremely shy before me. Therefore it was impossible for her to speak out if there was something bothering her. I tried to joke with her, plead with her, divert her attention to something else, but nothing seemed to work. Then my mother-in-law came to me and asked me a question. "Pastor Cho, do you enjoy living with my daughter?" I said I did, and she said, "Pastor Cho, if you keep to this path, you will lose my daughter."

"Why, what do you mean by that?" I said. "I treat my wife well, so what's the problem? We have a nice house; I buy her food to eat and clothes to wear. Where is the inadequacy? What more must I do? I'm doing fine as it is."

She stared into my eyes calmly, steadily, and said, "Look here, I see you don't understand. You haven't put a new piece of furniture in your house. You have not brought home any visitors. A human being cannot live with just a roof over their head, food, clothes, money, and nothing else. They need love, recognition, fellowship—that is what is lacking in your home."

I pondered this for a long time. I comforted myself by thinking, "This is happening because I am serving God faithfully. I am working for the Lord. Why must my wife require all this love and attention?" But my wife became more and more depressed, so I went out and prayed to the Lord. "Lord, I feel that I must choose between my calling and my wife. Bringing you glory and serving you is more important. If I must choose between the two, then my choice is to lose my wife. My calling to you is more important to me than my wife. God, perhaps my wife will suffer a sudden death, or maybe choose to live a life alone so that I might perform my service to you."

The Holy Spirit spoke gently to my heart: *"No, no, no. You have made a severe mistake in your priorities. Up until now you have put God first, church second, yourself third, and your wife last. This is a huge mistake. Of course, God must come first in your life, but your remaining priorities must be reexamined. Your own life must come second, and your wife must come third. If you have a child, this child will be fourth, and at the end must come the church."*

I immediately became frightened that I was hearing something that wasn't right, and I started examining the idea. I thought that it couldn't possibly be the voice of God. This was an incomprehensible notion from the perspective of East Asian culture. As I kept thinking it over, nearly rejecting what I heard, the Holy Spirit spoke to me again: *This is not an idea that has come from American culture or some other Western country. This is my method. God must come first. But you must come second, because in order for you to serve in this manner, you must live a holy life. Next must come your wife. If you were to lose your wife or divorce her, your words would no longer reach anyone's ears. Your ministry will continue to expand. You can build a great church, but if you lose your family, you will lose your entire ministry. Having an intimate relationship with your wife is more important than setting up a church. The entirety of the church depends on the everyday life of your family."*

I decided to meekly accept the words of the Holy Spirit. I gave up writing the literature for the evangelistic meetings, and I promised to spend every Monday with my wife. I told her that I would grant her whatever she wished on Mondays. If my wife wanted to go to the park, I would go with her; if she wanted to go to department stores to shop, I would go with her. In the evenings we would have a wonderful time just being together. And every morning I told her something like this, "I love you. You are so cute. You are marvelous. I am overjoyed just to have you beside me."

A miracle wasn't long in the making. My wife's depression started to disappear, her expression changed, and she started to regain her lost vigor. She began by carefully smiling, then she started to laugh, then her personality started to brighten enough for her to even make an occasional playful comment. She even started to prepare delectable dishes and handsome meals for me. We had delightful times of fellowship and made a wonderful, happy family. We made plans to pray together and serve together. It was during all this that I came to a new understanding. A proper family life requires true fellowship with each other. In particular, it is important to have fellowship with your wife above all else. A wife is more than an object, she is a wonderful, living, personality; even more, she is a lifelong partner and friend to be cherished.

Marriage to the Holy Spirit

The relationships husbands build with their wives are the same as the relationships every Christian must have with the Holy Spirit. Though the Holy Spirit is always with us, we cause Him much grief when we abandon Him to the dark corners of

Dr. Cho speaking at the Azusa Street Centennial celebration.

our minds and bring His name to light only for the Benediction or for the sake of theologically correct diction. When we do this, the Holy Spirit does not participate in our acts of service, and our very service itself will be barren and fruitless. Pastors may be theologically brilliant and the very picture of eloquence when they give their sermons, yet still be unable to produce spiritual fruit. Service to a calling that does not originate from the Holy Spirit is service of the flesh rather than the spirit.

When I realized all this, my relationship with the Holy Spirit grew immensely. The Holy Spirit must never be ignored, for He is here to help us in our service to the Lord. God sits on the throne, Jesus sits at His right hand, and the Holy Spirit lives within us to further the work of our King. I respect the Holy Spirit as the most important person in my life. I give praises to Him, and to Him I confess my love. "Holy Spirit! I love you. Together let us call out and pray to the Father and His Son Jesus Christ. And even when I read the Word, may you always read with me."

My fellowship always begins with the Holy Spirit. After that, I dedicate my services to God and Christ Jesus with whom the Holy Spirit always resides. Because I have such an intimate relationship with the Holy Spirit, whenever He speaks to me I listen and respond at once. If the Holy Spirit speaks of healing, I understand immediately. If He speaks of new construction projects, I understand. The Holy Spirit has a definite, tangible, existence to me. When I first wake in the morning, I spend time communing with the Holy Spirit. No matter what my plans are for the day, I like to spend one hour dedicated to Him. All my needs, I first request of the Holy Spirit. "Please conduct this upcoming meeting together with me. Please read this Bible together with me."

In this manner I work together with the Holy Spirit, give praises to God and Jesus, hold services, and study the Bible. I love the Holy Spirit and give praise to His name. All my services I plan and carry out together with the aid of the Holy Spirit. When the members of the early Church gathered publicly in Jerusalem, the Holy Spirit was in definite, direct, fellowship with them. Once they had been invited and gathered for the purpose of settling the question of how to deal with the question

Dr. Cho praying during a service.

of the circumcision of Gentiles. There came a definite answer. "It seemed good to the Holy Spirit and to us not to burden you with anything beyond the following requirements" (Acts 15:28). This decision came not from these men alone, but together with the Holy Spirit.

Could we say the same about our own church meetings? Could we say this of the business and ministry meetings of the church? When we record the minutes of the meeting, could we write "We decided together with the Holy Spirit?" We don't speak in this manner. We consider the Holy Spirit merely as an influence within our churches, within our meetings, and within our services to God. This is a colossal error.

The Holy Spirit has been sent to lead and guide us in everything we do for God and Christ. He is the intermediary between God and us. He is the overseer and chairman of our meetings. He is the supreme pastor, and we are simply his assistant pastors. We must always listen for His guidance in everything we do and obey His every word. Only in this way will we succeed in the work God has given us to do, and give honor and glory to our Lord Jesus Christ.

For fifty years the mighty Holy Spirit has enabled us to give help to the helpless and hope to the hopeless, and by so doing He has enabled us to build the world's largest church. May it always be to the honor and glory of God our Father, our Lord Jesus Christ, and the blessed Holy Spirit.